D1287069

From Klein to Kristeva

Critical Perspectives on Women and Gender

Critical Perspectives on Women and Gender brings books on timely issues and controversies to an interdisciplinary audience. The series explores gender-related topics and illuminates the issues involved in current debates in feminist scholarship and across the disciplines.

Series Editorial Board

Ruth Behar
Müge Göçek
Anne Herrmann
Patricia Simons
Domna Stanton
Abigail Stewart
Christina Brooks Whitman

Titles in the series

Michelle Fine
Disruptive Voices: The Possibilities of Feminist Research

Susan D. Clayton and Faye J. Crosby
Justice, Gender, and Affirmative Action

Janice Doane and Devon Hodges
From Klein to Kristeva: Psychoanalytic Feminism and the Search for the "Good Enough" Mother

From Klein to Kristeva

Psychoanalytic Feminism and the Search
for the "Good Enough" Mother

Janice Doane and Devon Hodges

Ann Arbor

THE UNIVERSITY OF MICHIGAN PRESS

BF
175.4
.F45
D63
1992

Copyright © by the University of Michigan 1992
All rights reserved
Published in the United States of America by
The University of Michigan Press
Manufactured in the United States of America

1995   1994   1993   1992   4   3   2   1

A CIP catalogue record for this book is available from the British Library.

Library of Congress Cataloging-in-Publication Data

Doane, Janice L.
    From Klein to Kristeva : psychoanalytic feminism and the search
for the "good enough" mother / Janice Doane and Devon Hodges.
        p.   cm. — (Critical perspectives on women and gender)
    Includes bibliographical references and index.
    ISBN 0-472-09433-5 (alk. paper). — ISBN 0-472-06433-9 (pbk. :
alk. paper)
    1. Psychoanalysis and feminism. 2. Object relations
(Psychoanalysis)—History. 3. Mother and child—History.
4. Femininity (Psychology)—History. 5. Klein, Melanie.
6. Winnicott, D. W. (Donald Woods), 1896–1971. 7. Chodorow, Nancy.
8. Kristeva, Julia, 1941–   . I. Hodges, Devon L., 1950–   .
II. Title.   III. Series.
BF175.4.F45D63   1992
150.19'5'082—dc20   92-36505
                                                              CIP

Acknowledgments

Our work, because it is coauthored, is explicitly collaborative. Yet the two of us are only a small part of the large group of people who have made this book possible. We have relied heavily on the generous assistance of others.

We would particularly like to acknowledge our debts to friends who gave up that most valuable commodity, time, to read and reread our manuscript. Steve Brown, Scott Derrick, Michelle Massé, and Tania Modleski offered invaluable suggestions that helped us to shape our argument more carefully. Though there is not space enough to acknowledge personally all of the friends and colleagues who offered sympathy and support, we want to mention a few of them: Denise, Barbara, Deborah, Nancy, Sandy, Glenna, Carol, thank you. We also received much needed institutional support. Jan would especially like to thank Dean Paul Zingg who provided valuable course-release time. The St. Mary's College of California Faculty Development Fund also supported her research and travel. Devon would like to thank George Mason University for research-release time. Both of us, of course, greatly appreciate the encouragement and advice we received from LeAnn Fields and others at the University of Michigan Press.

To our husbands, Eric and Jim, thanks for being "good enough moms." And thanks to Alex, Cecily, Sara, and Tristan for being so flexible that we were able to see the limits of parenting requirements that rigidly define what is "good enough."

Contents

Introduction

Recent feminist and psychoanalytic accounts of mothering have been profoundly shaped by the work of Melanie Klein, D. W. Winnicott, Nancy Chodorow, and Julia Kristeva. All of these psychoanalytic writers have in common a concern to understand object relations, that is, the child's relation to internalized "objects," most often the breast or the mother as the child's first caretaker. Because object-relations theory has profoundly influenced recent feminist discourse, we think it is crucial to ask a number of pertinent questions about it. What notions of femininity do these writers sustain? What views of motherhood do they endorse? What is "good enough" mothering? "Good enough" according to whom? How are standards of maternal propriety established and sustained?

Many feminist advocates of object-relations theory believe that it has encouraged a liberating focus on mothers and daughters, women's nurturing capacities, and maternal ways of thinking, all topics that mark a turn away from oppressive patriarchal systems. Other feminists share our concern that this quite marketable literature about motherhood is a sign of feminism's embrace of traditional notions of femininity at a time of cultural backlash against women's efforts to expand their domain beyond the home. It is our view that recent psychoanalytic feminism with precedents in object-relations theory does little to transform the forms of agency and subjectivity available to women. Much of the writing we analyze is implicitly or explicitly prescriptive: it defines femininity in relation to mothering and then establishes women's agency as a set of approved behaviors toward infants, infants whose "selves" are described as if there were no problem determining the contents of their unconscious.

Our challenge to object-relations theories in some ways echoes the concerns of other feminist theorists. We join with those feminists who have argued that object relations, and indeed psychoanalysis as a whole, ignores the mother's subjectivity. But to argue just that is not enough. An emphasis upon the infant's needs, assumed to be unproblematic, calls forth a description of a mother "good enough" to address these needs. What if one did not automatically assume a universal infantile need for parental mirroring? Is it indeed likely that, historically, the selflessness demanded by such mirroring (so apparently natural to the mother according to Winnicott) has ever been attained?[1] That these questions are so rarely asked is proof of the incredible power of the psychoanalytic tale of child development popularized by child-rearing manuals, promulgated by pediatricians, and perpetrated by social policy. Object-relations theorists and those influenced by them quickly forget the possibilities of historical and social analysis and context. Even someone as concerned about the social order as Nancy Chodorow tends to impose a fixed, seemingly universal meaning on the infantile unconscious. So, for example, when Chodorow "describes" the infant's desires, she actually reproduces Winnicott's oppressive narrative about those desires and the mother's obligations to fulfill them. Chodorow argues that the mother's internalization of sexual difference creates sexual difference in the child, but it seems more productive to recognize the extent to which our internalization of idealized parenting requirements is at work to preserve this difference. Perhaps feminists need to imagine that these parenting requirements do not necessarily promote the right response to real needs. The object-relations emphasis on early infantile experiences tends to deemphasize the role of culture and representation in constructing what otherwise may appear to be pre-linguistic entities such as the preoedipal period, infantile fantasy, and, often, gender itself. Because we focus on the language of object-relations theorists—not on the "truth" of the child's earliest fantasies of the mother or of the mother's "natural" responsibilities toward the child—we have placed ourselves outside the belief system of these writers.

But if our emphasis on discursive practices makes us critical of the universalizing assumptions of object-relations theory, this same emphasis also leads us to examine textual complications, contradictions, and uncertainties that make difficult a simple assessment of these writings as feminist or antifeminist. Klein's work, for example, insists that we take a paradoxical position toward her contribution to feminist theory. Klein never offers a sentimental representation of the infant or the mother. The Kleinian infant is sadistic, paranoid, depressed. By so constructing the infant, a result of insisting on the primacy of violent infantile phantasies,[2] Klein takes the burden of blame off mothers. Mothers, says Klein, can do little about the primitive emotions of their infants. Klein, thus, suggests that mothers are not responsible for all the vicissitudes of their children's lives, psychic and social. As mothers ourselves, constantly barraged by the contradictory demands associated with maternal propriety ("good" mothers should be selfless nurturers; "bad" mothers are selfless nurturers who merge dangerously with their children, to give but one example), we find Klein's refusal to regulate motherhood wonderfully subversive. Yet Klein *does* believe in "natural" sexual difference and the inevitability of the child assuming its "correct" sexual orientation. For her, homosexuality is a perversion and femininity, so fraught with difficulty for many of us, is simply *there* from the beginning. So, what is a feminist to make of Klein? Perhaps it is best to see Klein's work not as a unity that can be extolled or eschewed by feminists but as a complex discourse whose limits and possibilities can teach us something about that ongoing project of interpretation called psychoanalysis—and its uncertain relation to feminism. Even though Klein's work supports Winnicott's promotion of traditional notions of sexual difference, her work also helps us to resist Winnicott's genial but deeply normative platitudes about what constitutes "good enough" mothering.

We do not mean, however, to privilege Klein as the *really* right parent of object relations. To make Klein our "good enough" mother would be to preserve the hierarchical familial trope of conventional genealogical projects often so devastating in their placement of women.[3] Our genealogical project has other aims: to offer a close reading and analysis of primary materials, but to do so in the hope that the discontinuities revealed—the internal contradictions of individual texts as well as the misprisions of those influenced by them—will be illuminating. All object-relations theorists preserve the idea of the mother as origin; we hope to show how this "origin" and "cause" is, in fact, the *effect* of a discursive practice that itself has multiple origins. This discursive practice is a process of selective emphases; the insights of one generation are often recast to buttress the values of another. Even feminists intent upon questioning the mother's placement in psychoanalytic theory have participated in a selective reading of texts in order to recreate key authors as "good enough" feminist mothers willing to underwrite contemporary fantasies of maternity. In this respect, it is the *preservation* of originary assumptions rather than a series of departures or misprisions that has created a trap for feminists. There may appear to be a vast political difference between Winnicott's insistence upon "good enough" mothering and Chodorow's demand that fathers participate more in child rearing; we will demonstrate, however, that Chodorow's unwillingness to question the systemic assumptions of object-relations theory cripples her more progressive aims.

Our genealogy, then, hopes to trouble what has become a naturalized story about identity formation. We recognize that such a project is risky in the face of a contemporary, deeply felt need on the part of many feminists for a unified female identity around which to rally our much embattled forces. Yet, as Judith Butler reminds us, feminism has long been troubled about its own pronouncements: "Contemporary feminist debates over the meanings of gender lead time and again to a certain sense of trouble, as if the indeterminacy of gender might eventually culminate in the failure of feminism. Perhaps trouble need not carry such a negative valence" (ix). Butler suggests that it is precisely the mission of feminism to trouble gender categories that have been made to seem natural, foundational unities—including feminism's own favored constructions of masculinity and femininity. It seems particularly useful to keep Butler's remarks in mind when interrogating psychoanalytic theory, a theory important to many feminists and yet also implicated in the naturalization of sexual difference. Yet our point is *not* that psychoanalytic theory is necessarily conservative. We are analyzing a particular branch of psychoanalysis—object-relations theory—and we occasionally use psychoanalytic theory against itself in order to stir up trouble.

A genealogical project with an attentive examination of language can, for example, remind us of the ease with which psychoanalytic terms can become clichés, calling forth an automatic train of associations that become rigidly locked into place. Writing about this process in her recent book *Between Feminism and Psychoanalysis*, Teresa Brennan shows how, for example, an identification is often assumed between the "Symbolic," the "phallus," and the "father." As we will demonstrate, a similar equation is made between the "semiotic," "female desire," and the "mother." Brennan suggests that we scrutinize the history of such naturalized identities.

> To think fluidly about associated terms, and their difference rather than their similarity, they have to be unfixed; the grounds for their association re-examined. This re-examination is in some sense historical. To say this much is to assume only that the recovery of the course of debates and issues that compose the historical context leads to another perspective; it is not a claim that finding a context is ever final, merely that the process of trying for it is a corrective . . . reconstructing the story from its premises to see if things look different. (12)

Brennan places Lacan at the origin of debates about psychoanalysis and feminism; *From Klein to Kristeva* begins with an earlier figure, Melanie Klein, who influenced both Lacan and Winnicott. Winnicott, in turn, has had a significant impact on American feminist psychoanalysis, most notably articulated and popularized in Nancy Chodorow's writings. Of course we, too, tell only part of the story. Yet we hope that our reconstruction and repositioning of object-relations theories about the mother-child dyad will address Brennan's challenge to make "things look different" and encourage new thinking about the relation between feminism and psychoanalysis.

The three chapters of this text attempt to show how object-relations theory works as a gendering structure that underlies much recent feminist psychoanalysis. The first chapter, "From Klein to Winnicott: A New Mise-en-scène for Mother," offers a reading of the work of Melanie Klein and D. W. Winnicott that provides a critical summary of the way these influential theorists construct the mother and the infant. The second chapter, "The Uneasy Search for Alternatives," investigates Nancy Chodorow's object-relations account of female identity, an account that disturbingly frames the mother as an origin, yet supports a utopian myth of female relationships that literary critics have found very compelling. The last chapter, "Kristeva's Death-Bearing Mother," challenges the usual way of understanding Kristeva's relationship to object-relations theory. Instead of positioning Kristeva as a Lacanian analyst, we read her as an object-relations theorist who returns Lacanian theory to biological foundations. Indeed we argue that object-relations theory, as appropriated by Kristeva, is unproductive of a feminist politics. Not only has Kristeva attacked feminist practices as symptomatic of regressive psychic states in some of her articles, but in *Black Sun* she focuses increasingly on a psychic realm within which sexual difference is linked to nature rather than culture. Our narrative, then, does not fulfill expectations that it will follow a trajectory that, in moving from Klein to Kristeva, moves from less to more subversive discourses. From start to finish, we remain troubled about the way object-relations theorists, in their search to describe originary experiences, have shored up an oppressive identification of the "feminine" with the "maternal."

It might provide a wonderful sense of completeness and wholeness to our book if, after criticizing the work of object-relations theory, we presented a single "correct" view of mothering. Yet we hope our readers will see how dangerous such prescriptions are, and how important it is that women define maternal propriety situationally. Once we take seriously the importance of determinant social conditions, the construction of a timeless "good enough" mother seems a necessarily conservative gesture. Universalizing discourses about motherhood have benefited women very little. Despite the feminist impulse behind the revival of object-relations accounts of the mother-child dyad, the desire to elevate the mother has worked to define women narrowly as mothers, and to define mothers as the idealized and blamed origin of the child, the family, and the state. By making visible a small patch of the language that has constructed us as feminists, as well as defined women as mothers, we hope to give readers a chance to rethink and renegotiate the meaning of femininity.

Chapter 1

From Klein to Winnicott:
A New Mise-en-scène
for Mother

With the advent of object-relations theory, the mother, long relegated to the wings of psychoanalytic thought, moved to center stage. Her role in the child's development was emphasized to the point where her authority and power far exceeded the once all-powerful father's. Investigating the implications of this reversal has become the task of much recent feminist theory and, of course, our book as well.

Melanie Klein did much to initiate the development of the new "mother-centered" psychoanalysis and, with this new development, the school of object relations. Yet, unfortunately, her work has received little attention from American psychoanalytic feminists. The notable exception to this pattern of neglect is Dorothy Dinnerstein's *Mermaid and the Minotaur*, a book that never generated the immense interest accorded to Nancy Chodorow's *The Reproduction of Mothering* in which Klein is dismissed because of "Klein's, like Freud's, instinctual determinism" (124).[1] Chodorow, certainly the most influential feminist object-relations theorist, finds non-Kleinian object-relations theory to be more assimilable to feminism because it emphasizes what seems to be a social experience. Melanie Klein rarely describes the mother's interactions with the infant, focusing instead upon the infant's phantasies of the mother. Those object-relations theorists who departed from Melanie Klein, beginning with D. W. Winnicott, emphasize "social" interactions and relationships, specifically the give and take of the mother's exchange with her infant.

Chodorow's alignment of Klein's work with "instinctual determinism" and non-Kleinian object relations with the "social environment" has been readily accepted by many feminists. Yet describing Klein's work as "instinctual determinism" is far too reductive, while

7

describing Winnicott's mother-child dyad as a "social environment" is far too generous. By privileging the work of Winnicott, feminists can easily miss the more insidious ramifications for women of Winnicott's difference from Klein. In this chapter we will discuss the disjunctions and continuities between Klein's work and Winnicott's appropriation and redefinition of it. Winnicott replaces Klein's mise-en-scène (in which an active infant creates phantasies about the mother) with what he calls the "maternal environment" (in which most mothers "naturally" respond to apparently real infant needs). Despite Winnicott's rhetoric about the importance of the mother's role, his restaging of the mother's place in child development is hardly liberating for women.

By mapping the psychic terrain of the nursing infant, Klein changed the focus of psychoanalysis from the child's relation to the father to the child's relation to the mother. But while this focus on the mother-child dyad is precisely the terrain of so much recent feminist criticism, Klein emphatically did not posit some blissful symbiotic preoedipal stage, or even some mutually gratifying relational construct of the sort that would be extolled by later object-relations theorists. Indeed, the gratification of the nursling, which might arise from the pleasure principle, is subordinated in Klein's account to the aggressive anxieties, frustrations, and splitting that the infant experiences in relation to the breast. Klein claims that these responses to the breast arise from the death drive. In accepting the importance of the death drive, Klein was following Freud, who, in a late and still controversial move, established aggression as "an independent energy source in its own right and speculated about its origins in a pervasive biological self-destructive tendency he termed the death instinct" (Greenberg and Mitchell 123). Klein's formulation of the "paranoid-schizoid" position, the position occupied by the infant upon birth, depends for its elaboration upon this constitutional aggression of the infant: "We are, I think, justified in assuming that some of the functions which we know from the later ego are there at the beginning" ("Notes on Some Schizoid Mechanisms" 179).

According to Klein, the nursling's aim in the paranoid-schizoid position is "to possess himself of the contents of the mother's body and to destroy her by means of every weapon which sadism can command" ("Importance of Symbol-Formation" 219). The infant is motivated to both possess and destroy the mother not only by constitutional aggression but also because of a simultaneous perception of the mother as the source of all good things. Yet the mother is not simply a source of plenitude, given the infant's ability to fragment, in phantasy, the mother into "part objects"—milk, feces, breast, penis, children. By greedily introjecting good part objects, splitting them off from bad part objects (objects created by the infant's own aggression in the mirror of its own sadism), the infant defends itself in this position from complete disintegration. The bad objects are felt to persecute the infant—hence its paranoia—and this anxiety leads to the defenses of splitting, projection, and introjection. In turn, these defenses are vulnerable. For example, envy is described by Klein as a form of infantile aggression directed not toward bad objects but toward good ones (the "riches" of the mother's body). This primitive emotion may undo the defense of splitting by destroying the good object that is protected when the bad object is split off from the good object. No wonder, then, that the fundamental priority given to the infant's aggression and anxieties in Klein's work led Edward Glover to label the inner world of the Kleinian infant as a "matriarchal variant of the doctrine of Original Sin."[2]

The paranoid-schizoid position sets up its own vicious circle, whereupon the infant's greedy aggression fuels defenses that further compound this greedy aggression. The infant obviously will have great difficulty getting outside such a terrifying funhouse, a hall of mirrors constructed by the infant's own convoluted, threatening phantasies about the breast. In the Freudian account, a third figure, the father, intervenes to break up the relation between the mother and infant. In Klein's account, there is no third figure, but instead a new position—the depressive position—at which the infant arrives as a consequence of perceiving the mother as a whole person. In this position, there exists a phantasy of the *combined* parents. Hanna Segal describes this feature of Klein's theory: "This phantasy [of the combined parents] appears first when the infant becomes aware of his mother as a whole object but does not fully differentiate the father from her; he [*sic*] phantasizes the penis or the father as a part of his mother; his idealization of her makes him see her as the container of everything desirable, breast, babies, penises" (107). Though Segal does not label this phantasy as such, surely we can justifiably see it as the phantasy of the phallic mother.

In the "depressive position" the infant is able to integrate the previously split perceptions of the mother and perceive that there is only one mother with good and bad features. The infant feels anxiously guilty to preserve this new, whole object against his or her own aggressive and destructive impulses. The resolution of this depressive anxiety, and the guilt that accompanies it, is accomplished through "reparation," the repair of the mother through restorative phantasies and behaviors. It is important to note what motivates the child to move from the paranoid-schizoid position to depressive anxiety and finally to reparation: "Klein makes it very clear that the child's concern for others does not consist simply of a reaction formation against his destructiveness, nor is it simply anxiety deriving from dependence on the object. The concern for the fate of the object is an expression of genuine love and regret, which develops . . . along with a deep gratitude for the goodness the child has received from the mother" (Greenberg 126).[3] The new driving force within the infant during "reparation" is the anxiety to make the object whole again through love. As Klein puts it, "Along with the increase in love for one's good and real object goes a greater trust in one's capacity to love and a lessening of the paranoid anxiety of bad objects—changes which lead to a decrease of sadism and again to better ways of mastering aggression and working it off" ("Contribution to the Psychogenesis of Manic-Depressive States" 144).

Clearly there is a disjunction between the destructive "paranoid-schizoid" position and the reparative "depressive" position. In the paranoid-schizoid position the infant is fundamentally motivated by an *inherent* destructiveness and its guilt and fear in the face of that destructiveness; in the depressive position, the infant is motivated by an *inherent* capacity to love and so to construct phantasies that restore both mother and itself as "whole." It is also significant that, at this stage, the infant's dealings with reality and an "other" object become important—the infant's objects are no longer simply internal or internally motivated. Klein's focus on reparation in her later writings opens the way for Winnicott's much more extensive focus on external objects and the environment.

Psychoanalysis inevitably posits a tale of development, and it is important to pause at this point to consider the implications of Klein's two positions for the classical psychoanalytical account of development. In the first place, Klein's term *position*, rather than stage or phase, is meant to reflect a strategic grouping of anxieties and defenses that are not restricted to the earliest stages but can persist and recur throughout life. But the implications of her new formulation for the classical Freudian model are more far-reaching than this. In all psychoanalytic accounts, the child's development is constructed as the move away from the mother and toward the father. By emphasizing the primacy of the mother, Klein is led to correspondingly diminish the importance of castration anxiety, which is so crucial a turning point in Freud. For example, Klein writes that while she agrees with Freud that "castration anxiety is the leading anxiety situation in the male, I cannot agree with his description of it as the single factor which determines the repression of the Oedipus complex" ("Oedipus Complex" 417) and she insists that "though the girl at one stage assumes that her mother possesses a penis as a male attribute, this concept does not play nearly as important a part in her development as Freud suggests" (418).

To define this developmental process, recent psychoanalytic feminists commonly use the terms *plenitude* and *lack*. A maternal "plenitude" is posited as available in the "symbiotic" union between mother and child. This union is broken up by the father who introduces "lack" and language. Thus, arguments tend to emphasize either *lack* or *plenitude* as if these terms did not, in fact, require each other. For example, in a recent article, Klein is associated with a view of maternal "plenitude" that is placed in opposition to Lacan's work with its emphasis on maternal "lack." [4] We have avoided the terms *plenitude* and *lack* in our own discussion of Klein because they erase elements in Klein's work that challenge contemporary views of the mother-child dyad. In Klein's view, the mother's "plenitude" (her riches, which include both milk and penis) creates anxiety in the infant rather than bliss. Further, the infant's anxiety has little to do with castration, or "lack," as Klein's way of positioning the oedipal moment makes clear.

Klein moves the oedipal moment to successively earlier points, "eventually locating [its] origins in the first year of life, around the time of weaning" (Greenberg 122). If the oedipal moment begins at this early stage it must necessarily entail anxieties primarily concerning the mother—and the father only secondarily. In Klein's work, the oedipal struggle is subsumed and consequently redefined in terms of depressive anxiety and the attempt to restore the mother as a whole object. At Klein's developmental turning point, she emphasizes depressive anxiety rather than castration anxiety. As Klein puts it, "The infantile depressive position is the central position in the child's development" ("Contribution" 289). Moreover, since depressive anxiety is never fully overcome, the subject is never fully finished with the mother. Ultimately, the work of symbol formation, art and culture themselves, can be attributed to our attempts to make reparation, to regenerate the mother. Klein writes that "there is no doubt in my mind as to the far-reaching and lasting influence of every facet of the relation to the mother upon the relation to the father" ("Oedipus Complex" 418).

Because of Klein's insistence on the priority of the mother, and her skepticism about the centrality of the castration complex, it is difficult to understand how the infant could be motivated to assume conventional gender roles. Indeed, gender differences are not important to Klein until the moment when she must explain how the child eventually assumes its "correct" genital organization. At this point, Klein resorts to explanation by fiat. "Inherent unconscious knowledge of the existence of the penis as well as of the vagina," she writes, "encourages the child to make the appropriate choice of sexual object" ("Oedipus Complex" 409). At the moment of resolution, Klein, more than Freud, argues that biology is destiny. The girl simply "knows" she has a vagina and so will assume her natural femininity. The boy "knows" he has a penis and so will assume his natural masculinity. Heterosexuality is normal; homosexuality is a perversion. Because of the way that Klein constructs the resolution of the Oedipus complex, she prefers the concept of a "genital" phase to the concept of a "phallic" phase ("Oedipus Complex" 417) in which the castration complex is predominant. In Freud's work, as Juliet Mitchell has pointed out, castration or the lack of it becomes "the crucial dividing line between the sexes" and the value attached to the phallus, at this moment, reflects the cultural power of men in a patriarchal society (*Psychoanalysis* 87). Klein's view of sexual difference as genitally based is finally conservative. She reaffirms a binary relation between masculinity and femininity and insists on the innately heterosexual destiny of each sex. Her emphasis on the importance of the mother in infantile phantasy (her important contribution to object-relations theory) should not be mistaken as a reconceptualization of sexual difference. Even though it gives the mother more power within the child's phantasy, Klein's work provides no cultural explanation for sexual difference and the difficulty the girl has in establishing her "femininity."

Yet if there are problems with the way Klein wants to explain the resolution of the Oedipus complex, it may be significant that the bulk of her work is devoted to what she calls the early stages of the Oedipus complex, a time, she insists, in which sexual identifications are multiple and complex. Though in Klein's work the resolution of the Oedipus complex seems to depend on biological givens, she describes the psychic activity of the infant as remarkably ungrounded in any external referent. Descriptions of her work invariably rationalize what Klein depicts as the paradoxically "normal" hallucinatory mental life of the infant. To retain a sense of the gothic complexity of Klein's view of infantile phantasy, Klein must be quoted. This passage, describing the psychic operations through which the super-ego is created, provides a characteristic example of her voice.

> Since under the dominance of the oral libido the infant from the beginning introjects his objects, the primary imagos have a counterpart in his inner world. The imagos of his mother's breast and his father's penis are established within his ego and form the nucleus of his super-ego. To the introjection of the good and bad breast and mother corresponds the introjection of the good and bad penis and father. They become the first representatives on the one hand of protective and helpful internal figures, on the other hand of retaliating and persecuting internal figures, and are the first identifications which the ego develops. ("Oedipus Complex" 409)

Klein speaks of "objects," "imagos," "representatives," a language that stresses the distance between these figures and "real" people. Indeed, in her account the dynamic interchange between inner and outer in the infant's unconscious life so confuses boundaries that reality cannot be a fixed point of reference. As her somewhat disorienting description of the simultaneous processes of introjection and projection insists, objects both construct the subject and are constructed by it.

> The relation to internal figures interacts in manifold ways with the child's ambivalent relation to both parents as external ob-

jects. For to the introjection of external objects corresponds at every step the projection of internal figures on to the external world, and this interaction underlies the relation to the actual parents as well as the development of the superego. In consequence of this interaction, which implies an orientation outwards and inwards, there is a constant fluctuation between internal and external objects and situations. ("Oedipus Complex" 409)

While this fluctuation of phantasmic identities is dizzying, it does allow for possibilities of identification that a more clear and fixed articulation of identity, such as that provided by Winnicott, might foreclose.

In Winnicott's work, it is always clear who is the mother, who is the baby, who is the father. In his view of normalcy, the concept of a "me" and "not me" is managed without much difficulty. In Klein's work, not only are such distinctions difficult to maintain, but it is hard to say what Klein's view of normalcy is. Klein, as if aware of this problem, explicitly defended her use of material drawn from case histories of children with severe emotional difficulties to describe "normal" psychic mechanisms. In this, she says, she is following Freud, whom she quotes as writing "Pathology has always done us the service of making discernible by isolation and exaggeration conditions which would remain concealed in a normal state" ("Oedipus Complex" 370). But as the history of post-Freudianism has demonstrated, both Freud's and Klein's insistence that there is no simple boundary between the normal and the psychotic, between reality and phantasy, has been unpalatable to many followers of ego psychology and object relations.

Klein's emphasis is always upon the kaleidoscopic world of internal phantasy and relations to internal objects. Even if the infant is making attempts at reparation, the infant is doing so, ultimately, in phantasy rather than in relation to a real person. Yet Klein's use of the word "object" lends itself as well to the notion of an independently existing reality. For Freud, the drives only gradually become attached to objects through experiences of gratification. In contrast, the "object" for Klein is preconstituted, inherent in the organism's drives in the form of constitutional, universal knowledge and images. As we have seen, the infant simply "knows" about penises, breasts, and vaginas and need not rely upon any external experience of them.[5] Thus, for Klein, the external world of very young children is not initially a source of objects: "in the beginning, external reality is mainly a mirror of the child's own instinctual life . . . peopled in the child's imagination with objects who are expected to treat the child in precisely the same sadistic way as the child is impelled to treat the objects" ("Contribution" 233). Yet Klein did not completely neglect the effect of external reality and of real parents. In her later work on "reparation" in particular, she stressed the *beneficial* effect that parents could have on the seemingly boundless sadism and aggression of the child. Indeed, Klein "has a tendency to see bad objects as internally derived, that is, as arising from the child's own drives, and good objects as absorbed from the outside, from the ameliorative effect of the parents' ministrations" (Greenberg 135).

Klein's use of the word *object* (internal or external) depends upon a belief in an independently existing reality and so fundamentally revises Freud's notion of the object as arbitrary. As the editors of *Formations of Fantasy* point out in their preface:

> What object-relations theories hold in common is the presupposition of a world of "objects" preconstituted as always-already "there" for recognition. What is thereby left out is the *constitutive* role of representations, substantial and psychical, conscious and unconscious, in the cultural production of "reality." What results from this "post-Freudianism" is, effectively, a comforting (indeed, sentimental) *pre-Freudian* positivism. "Reality" again becomes the privileged, *prior*, term—applied only to the public realm and, along with this realm, segregated from the unconscious. Thus insulated from history, the "reality" of the mother-child relationship is installed as the transcendental "biological constant" at the heart of all representation. (Burgin, et al. 4)

As we have seen, Klein hardly ignores the constitutive role of phantasy in the early oedipal stages. But by naturalizing object choice as a biological constant, Klein is able to align the phantasies of the infant with a grounding "reality." In this way, Klein resurrects the positivist view of reality that her own elaborations of the role of phantasy render so problematic.

Except when discussing the resolution of the Oedipus complex, Klein emphasizes the interaction between the internal and external to the point where external reality, as a discrete entity, is radically lost. The infant is not relating to a *mother* but to an imago of the breast and to an imago of the penis. As Klein tells the story of the child's development, the infant introjects imagos, imagos that are from the outset already split into good and bad. The infant also projects imagos, that is, *representations*. "In consequence of this interaction which implies an orientation outwards and inwards, there is a constant fluctuation between internal and external objects and situations" ("Oedipus Complex" 409). Within the logic of such a system, it is impossible to establish a point of exit from infantile phantasies to install a transcendental constant. Klein struggles to find a way out— biological difference, reparation, and even, faintly, the "real" mother who might mitigate the child's phantasies of destroying or being destroyed by the object. But while Winnicott was able to transform these gestures into a set of comfortable, predictable relations between a "self" and a commonsense reality, Klein's emphasis on the processes of projection and introjection continually disrupt her efforts to posit a stable, external reality. "As regards normal personality, it may be said that the course of ego development and object relations depends on the degree to which an optimal balance between introjection and projection in the early stages can be achieved" (Klein, "Notes" 185). This phantasmic "balance" is strikingly more precarious than the utopian area of "play" that Winnicott later creates as a haven from power, desire, and representation. In Klein's account, this balance also depends more fundamentally upon the infant's management of its own internally constituted phantasies than upon the mother's activities.

Klein's "mother" is wonderfully difficult to place; she is both inside and outside, both male and female. This "mother," whether imagined as ideal or destructive, is not "really" good or evil: she is a fluid construction of the child's desires and anxieties. Nor is the "mother" fixed in a gender category since she is, in phantasy, often combined with the father, himself both an idealized and hated object. When, in what Klein calls the "depressive position," the child imagines the "mother" as a whole object, this does not mean that the child identifies a whole "real" mother. Rather, the child worries that his or her own destructive impulses might have destroyed this object. Acute feelings of loss and guilt induce in the child a desire to make reparation. Here the "good enough" child now manages, *in phantasy,* to reestablish the loved object and install it within his or her inner world.

Thus, although endowed with power by the child, the Kleinian mother herself does not do anything to provoke the infant's aggressive phantasies except simply to offer or withhold the breast. In this respect, the Kleinian mother is very different from Winnicott's "good enough mother." The Kleinian mother is not a person endowed with subjectivity. Klein's emphasis on the infant's phantasy life is so strong that she has almost nothing to say about "real" mothers and how they behave. The exception is a partly prescriptive essay, "Weaning," that was originally included in a collection of psychoanalytic lectures entitled *On the Bringing Up of Children.*[6] Though most of the article describes the phantasy life of the child, it also includes a "how to" section. When Klein begins to discuss what can be done to help the child during weaning, the essay gets its first footnote: "I have to thank D. W. Winnicott for many illuminating details on this subject" ("Weaning" 297). She explains that the baby has to be induced to take the nipple in just the right way to insure a good relation between the baby and the breast. (In a letter to Joan Riviere, Winnicott complains that Klein does not really understand what a "delicate affair" the presentation of the breast is ["Spontaneous" 95–96].) In "Weaning," Klein does seem to accept a Winnicottian view of maternal responsibility when she writes that "a really happy relationship between mother and child can be established only when nursing and feeding the baby is not a matter of duty but a real pleasure to the mother. If she can enjoy it thoroughly, her pleasure will be unconsciously realized by the child, and this reciprocal happiness will lead to a full emotional understanding between mother and child" (298). Elsewhere in Klein's work, remarks about mothering are rare, though Klein occasionally will remind the reader that the presence of a "real" mother is important. "The presence of the real, loving mother diminishes the dread of the terrifying mother, whose image is introjected into the child's mind" ("Infantile Anxiety" 92).

Klein's reticence about discussing maternal responsibilities is partly a measure of her conviction, irritating to many members of the British Psychoanalytic Society, that her role as an analyst is to analyze the unconscious, an unconscious that she believes is revealed in the infant's inborn aggressivity.[7] References to her patient's environments are cursory. In her work, one feels that an immense distance exists between psychic reality and social reality. Yet, since no theory of the mother and child can be constructed independently from cultural constructions of motherhood, Klein's way of positioning the mother and child obliquely speaks to her social experience. Klein was a mother with children and her reticence about prescribing maternal duties and obligations, as well as her construction of the infant as instinctively aggressive, is not innocent of involvement in her lived experience of mothering—and her desire to refuse her role. Klein's ahistorical infant world--constituted by projections and introjections—may itself be a product of history. Perhaps it was not only a shrewd theoretical insistence on psychic mechanisms that led Klein to disassociate the infant from the mother; Klein herself was disassociated from normalized femininity. She did not exist within the confines of womanhood defined as selfless motherhood.

Motherhood, that seemingly inevitable destiny for women, was a cultural imperative difficult for Klein to negotiate. About the late-nineteenth-century German culture into which Klein was born, Claudia Koonz remarks that "until 1908 [it was] illegal for women to attend gatherings at which politics might be discussed and . . . women [were barred] from earning university degrees" (25). Women's place was emphatically in the home. Klein's marriage to Arthur Klein in 1903, which provided economic security for her and her family, was followed a year later by the birth of her first child, a daughter named Melitta whose later quarrels with her mother became the stuff of legend.[8]

After her marriage, Melanie Klein did not actively rebel against her female destiny. Instead, she became "sick" with nervous disorders that frequently required her to leave her family so that she could seek "cures." Klein's able biographer, Phyllis Grosskurth, has much to say about the troubled relations between Melanie Klein and both her angry, domineering mother, Libussa, who often assumed the care of Melanie's family, and her rebellious daughter, Melitta. However, Grosskurth is curiously silent about the destructive effects of prescriptions that insist upon motherhood as women's only legitimate occupation. Klein's biography suggests how the lived experience of motherhood can give impetus to questioning idealized views of the mother-child relationship. In her theoretical writings, Klein effectively seals off—and escapes—her painful lived experience of motherhood, yet her description of infantile phantasy is a record of traumatic encounters between infants and mothers. Klein's infant is anything but a sentimental construction. Far from being sweet and loving, the Kleinian infant is anxious, sadistic, and, at best, guilty. Klein imagines the mother-child dyad—in phantasy of course—as based on a dynamic of persecution and remorse.

Grosskurth also has little to say about Arthur Klein. Is the father, occupant of the public sphere, simply assumed to be naturally absent from the sphere of women and children? That Melanie Klein was finally able to divorce Arthur Klein and embark on a career is un-doubtedly connected to the emancipation of women in Weimar Germany, an emancipation that the Nazis strongly opposed. Klein, hav-ing become interested in the psychoanalytic study of children (an area deemed "suitable" for women), moved to Berlin in 1921 and divorced Arthur five years later, just prior to her immigration to England.

D. W. Winnicott acknowledges Klein's influence in his article "A Personal View of the Kleinian Contribution": her theories enabled him to "work on the infantile conflicts and anxieties and primitive defenses" (175). But Winnicott is obviously uncomfortable with Klein's account of those conflicts and the terminology Klein used to describe them. He says of the "depressive position," for example, "I think this is a bad name" (176). Such apparently simple changes in terminology in fact entail a complete conceptual shift. When he changes the term "depressive position" to the "stage of concern," he transforms the infant's psychic reality from one of anxiety, guilt, and loss to one of acceptance, achievement, and integration. Klein and Winnicott use some of the same words to describe the "depressive position"—both speak of "guilt" and "reparation," for example—but the greed of the Winnicottian infant is highly qualified: "Greediness in an infant is not the same as greed" ("The Antisocial Tendency" 312). Greediness is not the same as greed, because, for Winnicott, infantile greediness is always to be understood as a kind of self-expression that, with the mother's help (what Winnicott calls "hold-ing"), transmutes into personal growth. The shift from Klein's con-cepts to Winnicott's recalls the romantic shift in sensibility when doctrines of Original Sin gave way to beliefs in the innate perfectibil-ity of the child. If the infant is always basically "good enough," then when there is trouble someone or something other than the infant is responsible. And, while both parents may inevitably be targets of rage because they cannot avoid being sources of frustration, the culpable party in Winnicott's work is only one parent, the mother.

It is in Winnicott's definition and conception of the mother as an active agent that he departs most radically from Klein's views. Again, he represents his shift as simply a semantic one; he is simply *adding* the concept of "environment mother" to Klein's idea of "object mother."

> It seems possible to use these words "object mother" and "environment mother" . . . to describe the vast difference that there is for the infant between two aspects of infant-care, the mother as object, or owner of the part object that may satisfy the infant's urgent needs, and the mother as the person who wards off the unpredictable and who actively provides care in handling and in general management. ("The Development of the Capacity for Concern" 75)

Winnicott's separation of "object mother" from "environment mother" becomes a permanent divorce. Winnicott may pay lip service to the idea of "object mother," but he is primarily concerned with the notion of a maternal environment and maternal responsibility. What is most subversive about Klein's work is placed at a "vast difference" from Winnicott's concerns and indeed in opposition to them. Winnicott effectively opposes phantasy and reality, unconscious and conscious, maternal sexuality and maternal caretaking, and even Klein's funhouse of interpretation with his concept of the management of transparent needs. The importance of infantile sexuality, always a troubling feature of Freudian psychoanalysis and perhaps particularly disconcerting in Klein's account of infantile sadism, gives way to a less threatening narrative about the infant's self. If the mother will simply "hold" the infant's environment, the infant's nascent self will develop properly.Winnicott's emphasis on development rather than on sexuality can be seen as helping to create the tradition of psychoanalyst/pediatricians who write "how to" books for mothers in which the role of the unconscious hardly needs to be acknowledged. Indeed, Dr. Benjamin Spock was asked to write his famous book for parents, *Baby and Child Care,* because the publishers, Pocket Books, had discovered that Spock was the only American pediatrician with psychoanalytic training. In the introduction to his book *Babies and Their Mothers,* Spock gives Winnicott some credit for the shape of his own career: "Winnicott's writings . . . helped to bridge the gap between pediatrics and the dynamics of child development" (ix).

At first it might seem that distinguishing the "object mother" from the "environment mother" empowers the mother by acknowledging her subjectivity and her work as nurturer. Yet, while creating mothers as agents, Winnicott simultaneously creates them as objects for the regulatory discourse of experts. Winnicott's transformation of Klein's work thus allows for the marketing of his own expertise as a pediatric psychoanalyst. Of course Winnicott himself was always insistent that he wanted to save mothers from meddling experts. He believed his work to be descriptive not prescriptive. Yet if we turn to Winnicott's cheerful BBC broadcasts, in which feminist critic Denise Riley finds Winnicott slipping into "conservative asides," a close reading discovers a systemic conservatism that results from Winnicott's emphasis on "real" mothers, as if motherhood is a fixed and natural category.[9]

In Winnicott's view, "good enough" mothering is natural, intuitive, and follows automatically from every little girl's experience of playing with dolls. As he says in one of his radio talks, "If a child can play with a doll, you can be an ordinary devoted mother" ("Man Looks" 4). He seeks this mother out because he confesses that he has "a deep driving propulsion" ("Mother's Contribution to Society" 123) to find and appreciate the ordinary good mother and to speak to her.[10] Why does he see this as important? How can he, a male specialist working in a scientific discipline, intervene in what is a female, natural relationship? If this relationship is natural, what is there to say? Moreover, why is it so important for him to say it?

Winnicott negotiates his difficult position by adopting what appears to be a benevolent stance.

> I was not specially out to tell mothers what to do, because they can get advice over details quite easily from Welfare Centres. In fact advice over details comes too easily, sometimes causing a feeling of muddle. I have chosen instead to talk to these mothers who are ordinarily good at looking after their own babies, intending to help them to know what babies are like, and to show them a little of what is going on. The idea is that the more they know, the more they will be able to afford to trust their own

judgment. It is when a mother trusts her own judgment that she is at her best. ("Baby as a Going Concern" 13)

But even in the process of explaining himself, Winnicott is mired in contradictions. Knowledge is dangerous when it gives mothers ideas that divert them from the realm of the natural, but somehow someone must still tell them "what babies are like" and "a little of what is going on" (13). Winnicott's solution is to give mothers knowledge that will reflect back to them what they already naturally know—to act as their mirror. He will not then *tell* them anything; he will not be prescriptive. And nonprescriptive reflective discourse has its own style; just as it mirrors the natural, it too is closer to the natural—oral rather than written. Winnicott speaks in radio talks to the mother who, he understands, is not "usually a learner from books" ("Mother's Contribution to Society," 127). As he sums it up, "A writer from human nature needs to be constantly drawn toward simple English and away from the jargon of the psychologist, valuable as this jargon may be in contributions to scientific journals" (127). Unlike Klein, whose Germanically-inflected language depended upon and even exaggerated psychoanalytic jargon and who explicitly insisted on the child's psychic life as a complex maze of representations, Winnicott claims for himself the voice of nature. He does this by acting as a mirror; he will reflect back what the mother does naturally in clear, simple, direct, natural English. He does this so as to help mothers trust *their own* judgment. He takes his cues from *them*, much as the mother does a child. In this respect, Winnicott embraces the role that Klein eschewed: he constitutes himself as a mother to an audience of mothers who are like infants. But speaking for the mother is only one way to surreptitiously control her. Another way is to speak on behalf of the infant.

Like Klein, Winnicott speaks as if he has privileged access to the infant's emotions. But the Kleinian infant with its powerful innate drives lacks a coherent ego, while the Winnicottian infant is a persistent little individual with its own ideas that a mother must respect. In a radio talk entitled "Their Standards and Yours," Winnicott says, for example, "The truth is (according to my idea) that almost from the start the new baby has his own ideas" (89); and he says, "Let each child develop his own right to dominate" (91). The assumption behind such representations of infantile autonomy is that the preverbal infant has a fully formed subjectivity, an assumption that apparently contradicts Winnicott's theoretical descriptions of infantile subjectivity as formed within the mother-child dyad. What becomes obvious from his radio talks, however, is that this apparently balanced dyad is, in fact, a hierarchical relationship. In "Their Standards and Yours," Winnicott counsels mothers to qualify their own desire for autonomy by surrendering some of their standards to the child's. In other words, Winnicott's concern is to represent the child's needs and rights.

Winnicott defends the child's rights because he is concerned about the infant feeling too dependent on the mother. Like the infant, as he imagines it, Winnicott fears dependence on "WOMAN." "If there is no true recognition of the mother's part, then there must remain . . . a fear of dependence. This fear will sometimes take the form of a fear of WOMAN, or a fear of a woman, and at other times will take less easily recognized forms, always including the fear of domination" ("Mother's Contribution to Society" 125). Winnicott is saying that the child is dependent upon the mother for its sense of autonomy, which it obtains as a result of the mother's "true recognition." In other words, autonomy is not explained as a result of the child's separation *from* the mother. Winnicott wants to see the mother-child dyad as full of possibility (his idea of the potential space, for example, defines the mother and child in a perfectly comfortable dynamic of "me" and "not me"), but this discussion of the fear of domination reveals how crucial it is for Winnicott to maintain the mother-child dyad as a closed, hierarchical system based on the domination of the mother by the infant. When the infant is dominant, this "natural" hierarchy secures the child's autonomous identity. When the mother is dominant, the child's growth is stunted. Here, Winnicott quells his anxiety about maternal domination in several ways: he normalizes a hierarchical relation of child to mother; he turns the child's dependency on the mother into autonomy by imagining a maternal gaze with no castrating power (this gaze mirrors "truly"); and he defines nurturing practices, through appreciative description, so as to naturalize women's submission and thereby hide his own efforts to enforce their submission.

What does Winnicott say in his talks to mothers? Listen. "You" are a woman and "the beauty of it is that you do not have to be clever, and you do not even have to think if you do not want to" ("Man Looks" 4). What you are doing is "real" and "natural." Your love for the baby is "a pretty crude affair" (5). It has led you to give up all other interests. You do this job best when you know nothing about it, but you need someone to tell you what you know, or you might doubt that you know it. You must be reminded, for example, that what you do naturally had better be done correctly because "you are founding the health of a person who will be a member of our society" ("Baby as a Going Concern" 14). You'd better pay attention because you learn what you already know about your baby during naps, "feed times," while "changing napkins" ("Getting to Know Your Baby" 10). You shouldn't let someone fool you into thinking that you, rather than the child, should determine breast-feeding times. Enjoy! "Enjoy all this for your own sake, but the pleasure which you can get out of the messy business of infant care happens to be vitally important from the baby's point of view" ("Baby as a Going Concern" 14–15). Relax. It all depends on you, but don't worry, because "each baby is a going concern" and only needs you to respond to its needs (15).

And how does Dad figure into this picture? Dad is a man so he can "never really know what it is like to see a bit of [his] own self, living an independent life, yet at the same time dependent. . . . Only a woman can experience this" ("Man Looks" 3). Dad must "be and stay alive" so he can protect and maintain the home ("What about Father" 84).[11] He can also take on the bad qualities of the mother by representing law and order, "the human being who stands for the law and order which mother plants in the life of the child" (83). Mother must see to it that the children have at least some time with Father: "I should say that it is the mother's responsibility to send father and daughter, or father and son, out together for an expedition every now and again" (86). The father's relationship to the child, then, is also the responsibility of the mother.

One can imagine Winnicott's audience of mothers listening to him, grateful for the way he was appreciating and idealizing the mother's activities but also worried about how they measured up. His talks insist that a complete woman is a mother not only completely devoted to, but also fused with, her infant: "Sometimes the urine trickled down your apron, or went right through you and soaked you as if you yourself had let slip, and you didn't mind. In fact by these things, you could have known that you were a woman"

("Man Looks" 4). Sometimes Winnicott lapses into the use of imperatives when describing what is supposedly natural. "Enjoy being annoyed with the baby when cries and yells prevent the acceptance of milk that you long to be generous with. Enjoy all sorts of womanly feelings that you cannot even start to explain to a man" ("Baby as a Going Concern" 14). Woman is here being instructed to drastically reduce her own pleasures to pleasures associated with the baby. Not only is a lack of pleasure in urine and yells a sign that "you" are less than a woman, but this failure of womanliness is also dangerous to the baby: "The mother's pleasure has to be there, or the whole procedure is . . . useless" (15).

Winnicott's description of mothering, which also precisely coincides with his description of womanhood, reduces the sphere of woman's possibilities, though it is meant to suggest that the mother's role is expansive with opportunity. At first glance, motherhood looks like a position of full subjectivity and it is the father whose position is lacking—his role is marginal in the care of the baby. But Winnicott's insistence on the fullness of the woman's role as mother requires the redefinition of such issues as freedom, autonomy, and desire. So women are told that their freedom consists in the move from their father's house to their husband's, where they are "free" to "arrange and decorate the way [they feel] like doing" ("Their Standards" 87). A woman becomes autonomous, Winnicott tells his mothers, only when she marries, because marriage allows her to feel "proud" and "to discover what she is like when she is captain of her own fate" (88). The father disappears from the scene as though none of this decorating and arranging were done for his benefit: he is a nuisance to getting things done *her* way, in *her* home. As captain of her fate, she will "no doubt" find it "far simpler to get the baby to bed before father comes home, just as it is a good idea to get the washing done and the food cooked" ("What about Father" 81). A woman's desire, finally, is reduced to the "pleasure" of domestic management and infant care. Winnicott is cheerfully constructing for women the familial domain that made Melanie Klein, and others like her, sick as a young wife and mother. A critic of theories of the family has described how the hothouse environment of the nuclear family creates good bourgeois individuals through an insistence upon the family's illusory autonomy from the public sphere and an adherence to traditional sexual roles (Poster). Mothers who live only in the separate sphere of the family are socially and economically dependent upon men, whose power is enhanced by this dependency.

These broadcasts, so apparently privileging the mother, serve to maintain the power of the father. The baby, too, would certainly seem to benefit as the recipient of all this selfless love. Yet we are familiar with the oppressive, if not potentially dangerous situations created by the mother's self-denial. In one of her case studies, Melanie Klein pointed out what could happen to a child whose mother was "too good." This case involved a two year old girl who refused to speak and was completely impassive in her relations with others. Klein suggested that the child needed to be separated from her mother "in order to activate anxiety" (Grosskurth 368). After a series of short separations from her mother, the child began to communicate with others. Klein's association of separation anxiety with linguistic ability clearly prefigures the Lacanian notion that the child's separation from the mother, enforced by the Oedipus complex, signals its entrance into the symbolic order. But Lacan's account requires an emphasis on the concept of castration (the threat that breaks up the mother-child dyad), an emphasis that Klein refuses. It also sets up an opposition between maternal and paternal spheres that is closer to Winnicott's work than Klein's. Winnicott insists that he speaks from the position of a "man," but he also must find access to the supposedly separate, inarticulate sphere of mother and baby if he is to describe it authoritatively.

In an early talk, "A Man Looks at Motherhood," Winnicott's opening discussion implicitly acknowledges the paradox behind adhering to the notion of separate spheres: by defining woman as radically other than man, a man cannot possibly understand either what women already know or what they need to know. How does a man find access to this sphere? Winnicott travels to this foreign place vis-à-vis the imagination and, moreover, he colonizes this sphere by appropriating the mother's techniques as his analytic techniques. Though it may seem as though Winnicott is doing something unusual and daring—transferring attention to the mother, daring to appreciate her "superiority," using "mothering" techniques as his own—i.e., taking for himself behavior associated with the feminine—it is the analyst who gains power by this journey, not the women he sets out to protect. Ultimately, then, it is Winnicott and the promoters of "mother's place" (one thinks here of Phyllis Schlafley) whose needs are best served. It is one thing to occupy the place of the mother as a successful discursive strategy and another to be voicelessly immersed within it.

In his paper, "The Mirror-Role of Mother and Family in Child Development" (where the family is not really discussed), Winnicott's examples are drawn from case histories of female patients.[12] These examples are meant to demonstrate both the debilitating effects of the bad mother and the good work of the therapist, whose task is to rehabilitate his patients by playing the good mother. The "good-enough" mother provides a metaphoric model for the therapist, who "reproduces the earliest mothering techniques" by recreating an environment of holding, regression, mutuality, concern—namely an environment of what Winnicott calls "management" rather than "interpretation." With these techniques, the therapist repairs the damage done by the bad mother. In his writing, Winnicott reveals a desire to play the good mother to his readers as well as to his patients. As a good mother, he seemingly refuses to impose an interpretation based upon the development of his own assertions. This gesture allows him to insist upon his views rather than analyze them.

Winnicott proceeds by presenting what he calls "illustrations." Readers are invited to enter a portrait gallery containing four pictures of women. Winnicott selects these particular pictures for our gaze because all of these women were in therapy, apparently because they had bad mothers. Winnicott's role, as he perceives it, is to be a passive reflector capable not only of eventually rehabilitating these women by allowing them to "feel real," but also of presenting to us a "real" picture of his patients. But because Winnicott participates in—and helps perpetuate—a culture in which women typically function as mirrors (a role apparently natural to good mothers) while men have the power to actively interpret, he has difficulty carrying out his intentions to be a good mother.

In his first illustration, Winnicott presents a woman who seems to be a good mother. She not only raised "three fine sons," but was a "good support" to a husband who had a "creative" job ("Mirror" 113). But, surprisingly, this woman was "always near depression" and, thus, "seriously disturbed her marital life" (113). With this observation, Winnicott unwittingly reveals the strains put on the good mother, and indeed, the havoc that this supposedly natural role causes. Yet Winnicott blinds himself to the debilitating effects of being a good mother. In an earlier article, for example, he was concerned to "pay tribute" to a condition of "primary maternal preoccupation" that he himself described as bordering on temporary insanity and illness. This illness, however, is "normal." Only the abnormal mother, who is, according to Winnicott, one who suffers from penis envy or has masculine identifications, takes refuge in a "flight to sanity" at this crucial stage in her infant's life. Yet the good mother in his "illustration" is not only exhausted and depressed, she also seems to unconsciously acknowledge that her role is artificial rather than natural. Only by "putting on her face" (i.e., applying makeup) can she meet her responsibilities (114). Winnicott finishes this illustration by telling us that his patient eventually developed a "chronic and crippling physical disorder" (114).

Winnicott states that this woman's problem was that she "had to be her own mother" (114). Though he does not say so, we might assume that she had a bad mother, or perhaps no mother. But it seems more likely that she suffers because men, in Winnicott's view, cannot be mirrors, and she is surrounded by men. Winnicott tells us that "if she had a daughter she would surely have found great relief" (114). Unfortunately, she had only "three fine sons," a husband, and a therapist who apparently was also unable to be a "good enough" mother. Although he does not explicitly say so, Winnicott reveals here his own uncertainties about his ability, even the possibility, of his being a good mother. And, indeed, in his article "The Anti-Social Tendency" Winnicott claims that the analyst cannot treat the child for anti-social tendencies because only real—not therapeutic—mother-love will do. He also writes in "What about Father" that "there are some fathers who really would make better mothers than their wives, but still they cannot be mothers" (82).

Though he professes to want the role of the good mother, Winnicott continues to act as what he calls the "bad mother." He asserts his beliefs and constructs interpretations of women that establish his authority. The role of the bad mother is, in fact, empowering. So why insist on the primacy of the good mother? The answer is that the perpetuation of the idea of the mother as mirror sustains his role as therapist: the therapist gains therapeutic power by adopting a passive, benevolent guise. For women, Winnicott's idealized requirement that mothers live as mirrors ensures at best a feeling of inadequacy, and at worst, depression and illness, as his own "illustrations" reveal. And, too, freezing motherhood into a fixed, ahistorical category also obscures the diverse and changing needs of women as workers and reproductive social beings in a multicultural society. In Winnicott's construction of mothering, all mothers are married, at home, and happily defined by their maternal capacities. But this is neither how it is, nor how it was during the time of his broadcasts. During the war, women's participation in the work force increased and fathers were absent too, not through choice but because of wartime activities. After the war, most white, middle class women with young children gave up their temporary jobs and returned to the home, undoubtedly encouraged by the expert advice that it was good for children to be tended by full-time mothers—though grueling working conditions also may have had a role to play. Many other women continued to work, though, and these women were rendered invisible, or culpable, by a psychoanalytic discourse that denied the diversity of women's experiences, needs, and desires. In her book *War in the Nursery*, Denise Riley discusses postwar pronatalism in detail and remarks, "Without looking at this emphasis on the artificially isolated figure of the mother, conceived in a strikingly restricted way, it is not possible to grasp the long reaches of a psychology which relied on a nonemployed mother at its heart" (7).

As our review of the work of Klein and Winnicott shows, there are significant differences within this discourse of child psychology. Klein's theory of the child so marginalized the "real" mother as the innocent stimulus of infantile processes of introjection and projection that she remains a figure almost empty of agency and subjectivity. Winnicott makes the spectral Kleinian mother into an agent, but one who "naturally" denies her own agency: she *desires* to be without subjectivity so that she can be used as a living mirror by the child—and by Winnicott himself. The male therapist, not the female one, had the most to say about mothering. Indeed, Klein, who was "really a mother" had, according to Klein's biographer, "acknowledged that she was not a natural-born mother," while Winnicott, a man who had no children, is commonly perceived to have "possessed . . . a strong maternal identification" (Grosskurth 233). This maternal identification was, as we have suggested, an identification with a conveniently idealized mother as therapist. Yet, of course, it was Winnicott who argued for the naturalness of female nurturing capacities so as to preserve his own prerogatives as patriarch: selfhood, power, discourse.

The differences between Klein and Winnicott are striking in other ways. Klein lived a life marked by the experience of exile and otherness: she was a woman, a Jew, a German who had lived in Germany, Austria, Hungary, and England. Winnicott always belonged. He was born into a prosperous English family and inherited the privileges of the upper-class, white, Christian male. He was drawn to Klein as the innovative matriarch of British psychoanalysis, whose play technique seemingly allowed her to communicate with the psychic life of the child, and finally broke with her because Klein refused to accept his ideas about real mothering as an extension of her ideas about the role of the breast. How could she? That she claimed she was "not a natural-born mother" reveals both the extent to which she had internalized her culture's prescriptions for women (prescriptions reinforced by Winnicott) and her desire to reject those prescriptions. Furthermore, her complex conception of the infant's psychic life takes into account the role of representation and phantasy in a way that Winnicott's description of the infant's subjectivity does not.

By effacing the work of Klein and privileging the work of Winnicott, it has been easy to miss a radical shift that leaves psychoanalytic understanding of the role of phantasy and the unconscious behind in favor of an emphasis upon reality and normalcy. Winnicott's subtle shift in language from Klein's "object" mother to his own "environment" mother begins to focus our attention on the activities of a real mother, activities that soon become obligations—not so difficult to fulfill since they are also perceived as natural. Though the use of the word "environment" may seem progressive in that it acknowledges the importance of outside agency, Winnicott's "environment" was always too narrowly defined; even when this environment is extended, it remains linked to the mother as origin. Winnicott's formulation of the relation of the public sphere to the mother-child dyad makes this clear. As he puts it, "One can discern a series—the mother's body, the mother's arms, the parental relationship, the home, the family including cousins and near relations, the school, the locality with its police-stations, the country with its laws" ("Anti-Social Tendency" 310). One could add that other Winnicottian concepts such as the "transitional object" or "potential space" (Winnicott's name for the intermediary space between the mother and child) are just other points in this series, that is unidirectional and teleological.

Discussions of the maternal role always exist in an ideological framework in which they are purveyed to particular groups at particular times. In our own historical moment, analogies are often made between the family and the nation with vaguely articulated "family values"—often hostile to many kinds of family—widely endorsed. Ideas of maternal propriety have returned with a vengeance. In custody battles, experts now debate whether or not women are "good enough" mothers and Winnicott's way of positioning the mother's responsibilities have encouraged the view that "good" mothers find "their whole self" at home with children ("Their Standards and Yours" 88). More recently, the concept of "maternal environment" has been extended—to protect not just the best interest of infants and children, but also "fetal rights" and even the rights of children not yet conceived—all at the expense of the mother, whose own expression of self-interest, no matter how limited, is perceived to be a hostile act of aggression against her infant. Writing about this contemporary phenomenon in her book *Backlash*, Susan Faludi points out that antiabortionists skillfully manipulate language to reduce the pregnant woman to her womb and to elevate the fetus to full personhood. "The fetus is a conscious, even rambunctious tyke, the mother a passive, formless and inanimate 'environment'" (421). Faludi goes on to demonstrate in devastating detail that the reduction of women's possibilities to the one obligation of providing a "maternal environment" has literally cost women jobs, their wombs, and even their lives. At present, when technologies of reproduction are dramatically changing our notions of what have seemed unchangeable biological realities, what remains intact are prescriptions for mothers. Klein eschewed that tradition; Winnicott encouraged it.

Our responsibility as feminists is to analyze how these important theorists made use of language, psychoanalytic ideas, and their specific social position to shape our views of the mother-child dyad. A reevaluation of Klein's heterogeneous work might remind us of both the conservative force of psychoanalysis and the value of its most radical insight: the operation of the unconscious and fantasy is constitutive of our reality. This insight is a powerful tool, however, that cuts two ways. On the one hand, it might help explain the apparent intractibility of fantasies that contradict the actuality of diverse lives: Winnicott's idealized nurturing mother, for instance. But, as feminists, we too can fall prey to the fantasy or desire for an idealized mother. In this chapter we try to keep alive the contradictions and inconsistencies of Klein's texts that would prevent an easy privileging of her work to Winnicott's while also demonstrating the way in which Winnicott's agenda has been simplified to its seemingly most progressive aspects. In the next chapter, we move to another psychoanalytic "mother" of feminism, Nancy Chodorow. Much like the two theorists we have just discussed, Chodorow uses her psychoanalytic precursors in selective ways in order to revise them; her work, in turn, is reduced to only part of its message.

Chapter 2

The Uneasy Search
for Alternatives

It would be hard to exaggerate the centrality of Nancy Chodorow's *Reproduction of Mothering* and the extent of its influence on American contemporary thought. In order to explain the sexual division of labor, Chodorow argues that the child's early identification with the mother establishes a difference between masculine and feminine identities that encourages the reproduction of traditional social roles. Many recent feminist theoreticians use Chodorow's argument to ground their own, often celebratory, analyses of women's *different* social and psychic position. Carol Gilligan's popular *In a Different Voice*, for example, reproduces Chodorow's emphasis upon the mother-daughter relationship to account for differences in women's and men's morality. Philosophers Sara Ruddick and Jane Flax, legal scholar Robin West, and scientist Evelyn Fox Keller are other prominent feminist scholars who rely upon Chodorow's theory to distinguish men's and women's ways of thinking. In literary studies, Chodorow has shaped the psychoanalytic interpretations of such feminist critics as Judith Kegan Gardiner, Marianne Hirsch, and Claire Kahane, all of whom hope to define an authentic female voice.[1]

Chodorow, however, is not a simple origin for the ideas about masculine and feminine identity that her work has helped disseminate. Chodorow grounds her analysis in object-relations theory, using the work of D. W. Winnicott as well as the work of his followers, Michael and Alice Balint, W. R. D. Fairbairn, Margaret Mahler, Harry Guntrip, and others, all of whom focus on the importance of the maternal environment. Chodorow's contribution, as she sees it, will be to bring object-relations theory "to bear upon the question of gender" (*Reproduction of Mothering* 54; all further references to this work will be indicated by *RM*). Yet our analysis of Winnicott's work shows that a patriarchal gender ideology already shapes the concepts of "mother," "infant," and "self" crucial to non-Kleinian object-relations theory and Chodorow's own discourse. Winnicott's basic assumptions about what a child needs are uncritically adopted by Chodorow. Inevitably this appropriation leads to an insistence on the mother as the idealized and condemned origin of the child's identity and of the oppressive social system that Chodorow seeks to change. Chodorow's feminist analysis of culture founders on her assumption that object-relations theory can be made into a feminist theory simply by taking its developmental story and asking how it could work for girls.

Chodorow devotes the largest portion of her book to telling, as she entitles this section, "The Psychoanalytic Story." How and why she tells that story is worth examining. Chodorow relies on psychoanalysis because it shows the importance of unconscious processes in the formation of identity, and she is interested in the internalization of social structures. In the first part of her condensed history of psychoanalysis, Chodorow explains that in the theories of Freud, Klein, and ego psychologists unconscious processes are closely linked to aggressive and libidinal drives. She argues that as a result of their emphasis on innate drives, these theories make biology, rather than culture, the bedrock of psychic development. Here Chodorow effaces the distinction between Freud and Klein in order to unite and dismiss them. Klein, the founder of object-relations theory, is now aligned with Freud *against* object-relations theorists. As Chodorow sees it, object-relations theory (by which she means non-Kleinian object relations) provides an alternative, more cultural account of psychic development that emphasizes the way infants "transform drives in the course of attaining and retaining relationships" (*RM* 48). Explicitly, this history establishes a problematic opposition: Freud and Klein are to object-relations theorists as nature is to culture. Chodorow believes object-relations theory is particularly amenable to social theory because "object-relations theorists argue that the child's social relational experience from earliest infancy is determining for psychological growth and personality formation" (*RM* 47). Yet what object-relations theorists mean by "social relational experience" is the preoedipal mother-child dyad. Although Chodorow believes that object-relations theory is an advance over other psychoanalytic theories because of its emphasis on "social relational experience," object-relations theory actually mystifies the social construction of the mother-child dyad by defining that dyad as an origin.

Let us look at how Chodorow reproduces mothering as defined by object-relations theory. Winnicott's "environment mother" effaces her subjectivity and desire in order to serve as the ground of the infant's self. Chodorow acknowledges that there is a problem with descriptions of the mother which make it seem necessary that the mother's interests coincide with the infant's. Perhaps, she says, psychoanalytic theories fail to recognize potential conflicts of interest between mother and child because "these theories reproduce those infantile expectations of mothers which they describe so well" (*RM* 82). Chodorow's use of the words *reproduce* and *describe* reveal her assumption that these infantile expectations are "real." Do infants really expect the behaviors that Winnicott asks mothers to perform? Perhaps theories like Winnicott's *create* the infantile expectations that "they describe so well," and in so doing, legitimize efforts to regulate what women do.

According to Winnicott, as we discuss in chapter 1, the emergence of the infant's self requires "good enough" maternal care. Chodorow shows the extent to which she has uncritically assimilated his views about what constitutes "good enough" mothering when she writes that she does not "mean to raise questions about what constitutes 'good enough' parenting" (a phrase that inevitably collapses into "good enough" *mothering* not only because, as Chodorow knows, women have primary responsibility for infants but because the phrase derives from Winnicott's always gendered usage) (*RM* 22). *The Reproduction of Mothering*, then, simply reproduces what object-relations theorists say about the maternal role, a discourse that naturalizes and thus enforces requirements that are difficult for women (invariably understood as mothers) to fulfill. In a long section entitled "The Maternal Role," Chodorow explains the "selflessness" and "delicate assessments" that characterize good maternal behavior. Without any irony, she describes how a "good enough" mother serves the development of a child.

She needs to know both when her child is ready to distance itself and to initiate demands for care, and when it is feeling unable to be distant or separate. This transition can be very difficult because children at this early stage may one minute sense themselves merged with the mother (and require complete anticipatory understanding of their needs), and the next, experience themselves as separate and her as dangerous (if she knows their needs in advance). The mother is caught between engaging in "maternal overprotection" (maintaining primary identification and overdependence too long) and engaging in "maternal deprivation" (making premature demands on her infant's instrumentality). (*RM* 84)

Chodorow quotes Winnicott's description of the "magic" mother: "If now [when the child is capable of giving signals] she knows too well what the infant needs, this is magic and forms no basis for object relationship" (*RM* 84). While Chodorow says that the mother is "caught" by the paradoxical demands on her attention—she must be both omnipotent and blind—the tone of the passage is otherwise unforgiving of maternal lapses into a nonmagical realm of interpretive difficulty. Chodorow writes: "The ability to know when and how to relinquish control of her infant, then, is just as important as a mother's initial ability to provide total care" (*RM* 84).

This endorsement of Winnicott's "good enough" mother constitutes the most conservative moment in Chodorow's book. The "good enough" mother is not just "good enough," she is close to godlike. The Chodorow who embraces this idealized mother conflicts with the Chodorow who recognizes that the mother has commitments beyond caring for an infant.[2] Pointing out that the mother's point of view is ignored in object-relations theory, she nonetheless writes, "Analysts do not consider their prescriptions difficult for most 'normal' mothers to fulfill" (*RM* 85). Her use of quotes here would seem to indicate some skepticism about using the word *normal*. But at this crucial point, Chodorow's distinction between herself and male object-relations theorists is so fine as to fade into oblivion. Male theorists, she says, take "normal" maternal requirements for granted. She, on the other hand, believes that they are constructed—i.e., constituted within the mother-infant relationship (and by extension, so deeply embedded in women's psyche that they are not *difficult*). Moreover, these requirements are finally *necessary* to the child's proper development: "the analysts," she writes, "point to important characteristics of the mother-infant relationship and to necessary maternal (or parental) capacities" (*RM* 87). By accepting as necessary "normal" maternal requirements and "normal" infant demands as they are constituted in object-relations theory, Chodorow confuses her own argument. If prescriptions for "good enough" mothering are *not* difficult for "normal" mothers to fulfill, then why do women want men to share parenting responsibilities? And why do men refuse? Because of the way object-relations theory constitutes what is "normal," these questions are impossible to make from *within* object-relations theory.

Chodorow is aware, as Winnicott is not, that it is worth discussing why men rarely mother. Obviously, we think that a prescriptive psychoanalytic discourse, such as that produced by Winnicott, works to normalize women's confinement to the home. Chodorow's reliance upon Winnicott thus undercuts her calls for a change in the sexual division of labor. Instead of criticizing requirements for child-rearing that are designed to drastically reduce the scope of activity for both women and children, Chodorow wants "good enough" mothers *and* "good enough" fathers. As much as feminists would like to see fathers share the work of caring for children (and work is required to rear children no matter how the nature of that work is defined) it does not seem necessarily liberating to involve both parents in "total care."

Since Chodorow cannot question requirements for parenting, she turns to a different question: why can't men do what is so "easy" for women and "necessary" for the child? "All people have the relational basis for parenting if they themselves are parented. Yet in spite of this, women—and not men—continue to provide parental (we call it 'maternal') care. What happens to potential parenting capacities in men?" (*RM* 88) To answer this question, Chodorow expands on Winnicott's idea of the mother as agent by arguing that mothers treat daughters differently than sons, identifying more and for a longer period of time with their daughters. It is precisely this longer period of identification that leads to a daughter's greater relational capacities, capacities that, in turn, better qualify her to be a mother herself.[3]

The linchpin of Chodorow's argument, then, is the mother's differential treatment of the girl and the boy child. Without differential treatment on the part of the mother, we do not get gender difference in infants. Chodorow admits that there is no firm empirical evidence to support her claim: "It is not easy to prove that mothers treat and experience differently preoedipal boys and girls. Maccoby and Jacklin, in the currently definitive review of the observational and experimental literature of psychology on sex differences, claim that the behavioral evidence—based on interviews of parents and observations of social science researchers—indicates little differential treatment" (*RM* 98). In place of empirical evidence, or of other theoretical accounts of sexual difference, Chodorow utilizes the biases of object relations to support her claim that mothers treat daughters and sons differently. Chodorow's apparently "new insight" about this differential treatment is very much bound up in the old logic of object relations. As did Winnicott, Chodorow creates the mother as an origin so that the mother's agency seems the key to her own oppression (the sexual division of labor). And in addition to reconstituting the mother as an origin, Chodorow recreates the implicit gendering of the infant in object-relations theory.

In his BBC broadcasts, Winnicott always refers to the infant as "he," a stylistic convention that also assumes the male child's "natural" prerogative to develop an autonomous self. When Chodorow adopts Winnicott's developmental sequence, she is adopting a gendered story whose assumptions she fully realizes in her account: boy children, she explains, have more bounded, autonomous selves than do girl children. What is the news here? The news is that this is an advantage to the girl because the boy's bounded, autonomous self is a defensive construction and for that reason unstable. According to Chodorow, women's mothering provides children with a core "female" identity that girls maintain and boys must repress. She cites the work of Robert Stoller to support this claim. "Stoller argues that both core gender identity and basic morphology may be best understood as female for both sexes" (*RM* 151).[4] Femaleness here becomes a solid entity, a fixed "core," while masculinity is a secondary and reactive construct. Chodorow complains that Freud and Klein are biologistic; but Chodorow's notion of a preoedipal gendered self born of the mother-child dyad drastically reduces the role of culture. If female identity is an irreducible core, then what role can be given to society, history, and language in shaping the subject position of women? In place of these cultural forces stands a lone figure, the mother. Furthermore, Chodorow's account of sexual difference makes gender identity seem surprisingly less malleable than it does in Freud's account, an account that allows for bisexuality, the disruptions of the unconscious, and the difficulty of achieving and maintaining a gendered identity.[5] While object-relations theory tells a story of the development of identity that weakens the importance of the oedipal moment, most analysts of this school still rely on the

Oedipus complex to account for sexual difference. But because, for Chodorow, "the girl has a fundamental sense of being female," those issues that "Freudians make the center of their account—penis envy, love for the mother, the very circuitous path to the normal feminine Oedipus complex with father as love object" become weak, secondary formations (*RM* 151). In Chodorow's view, the Oedipus complex merely exaggerates the differences between the "relational capacities" of girls and boys (*RM* 166). Chodorow agrees with other analysts that the daughter's attachment to the mother is a strong one, but for Chodorow, the little girl has a core feminine identity that is never abandoned; in the oedipal phase she does not change anything, instead she simply adds love for the father to love for the mother. "As we have seen, a girl does not turn absolutely from her mother to her father, but adds her father to her world of primary objects. . . . This means that there is greater complexity in the feminine endopsychic object-world than in the masculine" (*RM* 167). Since Chodorow conceives of gender identity, the core female self, as *primary* and genital heterosexuality as a secondary formation, she argues that the Oedipus complex is not as traumatic for the little girl as it is depicted in the Freudian account. As Chodorow describes it, the little girl assumes heterosexuality to gain some autonomy from her primary love object—her mother—rather than to make up for a lack. The father is a "symbol of freedom from this dependence and merging" (*RM* 121). In the oedipal drama, Chodorow finds a firm feminine self (to which love of the father is simply added) where other theorists have found loss, anxiety, and resistance to the fixing of gender.[6]

In Chodorow's account, the girl's early perception of the mother as too complete, not as wounded or lacking, persists into the oedipal period. The girl, in turning to the father, does not repudiate the mother but ultimately *gains*, by this turn, a richer endopsychic life than is available to the boy who must "precipitously" renounce the mother (*RM* 135). So, one could ask, why are women unhappy? As Chodorow tells the story, the girl child's fantasy of "the 'phallic,' active mother" (*RM* 120) never gives way to the discovery of women's, and particularly the mother's, relative powerlessness. This view of maternal plenitude is, inevitably, a response to the Freudian argument that women are lacking. In the Freudian account, the Oedipus complex begins with a child's realization that the mother is lacking something. Lack comes to define the meaning of sexual difference. In this story, power is associated with the paternal phallus, which the little girl desires. Freud's patriarchal discussion of the formation of gender identity—patriarchal both in its emphasis on the father's power and in its normalizing of that power—makes it necessary to confront how the inscription of sexual difference and male dominance are linked. Chodorow's narrative makes it all too easy to forget why women resist the cultural construction of feminine identity and sexuality.

The value of an early feminist psychoanalytic account of female development, such as Juliet Mitchell's in *Psychoanalysis and Feminism*, is that it shows how the institution of the father's law in the Oedipus complex explains the perpetuation of unequal power relations. Mitchell asserts that in the "situation of the Oedipus complex . . . the little boy learns his place as the heir to this law of the father and the little girl learns her place within it. . . . Freud always opposed any idea of symmetry in the cultural 'making' of men and women. A myth for women would have to bear most dominantly the marks of the Oedipus complex because it is a man's world into which a woman enters; complementarity or parallelism are out of the question" (403–4). By making the mother more important to the infant than the father, Chodorow reverses traditional explanations of power relations that have emphasized the father's role in the construction of sexual difference. In her account, the mother becomes the dominant figure and this has the effect of masking women's subordination, precisely the subordination she is supposedly explaining.

Yet how can we consider the mother as the dominant figure given the way her role is constituted by Winnicott, and by Chodorow who endorses his concept of the "good enough mother"? The list of necessary parenting capacities endorsed by these object-relations theorists reads like a job description for women in this culture. The role calls for people who are relatively powerless, who are willing to "identify" their interests with the interests of an infant, who are selfless, who are always aware of another's needs and willing to make those needs a priority. As Roger Gottlieb points out, "we need not offer a psychological explanation of the fact that women do this difficult, demanding, underpaid and often unrecognized labor—any more than we need a psychological explanation of the fact that in advanced industrial countries racial and ethnic minorities do the worst-paid and most unpleasant jobs" (104).

Gottlieb makes a good point here, but in his emphasis on a social explanation for women's mothering, he misses an important contribution that Chodorow intends to make. Chodorow wants to explain how women's psychic investment in mothering maintains the sexual division of labor. Many critics of Chodorow have not given her credit for attempting to explain women's role in their own oppression. Because of her reliance on Winnicottian object-relations theory, her explanation ultimately privileges the mother-daughter relationship and an essential feminine identity even though Chodorow remains critical of the social order that relationship is said to maintain. (Later, in our discussion of the work of Julia Kristeva, we will see how another theorist attempts to explain women's psychic investment in mothering.) What has made Chodorow's book popular is neither her critique of the sexual division of labor nor her concern about women's role in perpetuating that division. Instead, feminists have lauded Chodorow's appreciation of mothering as formative of women's identity. By examining one of the many distilled versions of *The Reproduction of Mothering*, we can quickly see how feminists have defined the "essence" of Chodorow's theory, as well as what they have decided to ignore. We have selected a summary of Chodorow's book by Sharon O'Brien because it is clear, detailed, and seems to carefully and fully describe Chodorow's argument. In representative fashion, O'Brien's summary also uncritically emphasizes the psychological aspects of Chodorow's argument.

Arguing that classic Freudian theory is inadequate in explaining female psychological development both because of its male bias and its stress on the oedipal period as the crucible in which adult personality is formed, Chodorow contends that mothering by women results in asymmetrical personality development in women and men: women tend to define themselves in relationship to others, whereas men do not.

According to object-relations theory, the infant's earliest relational experience with its mother structures its later development. The infant's original state is one of fusion with the mother who satisfies its needs for warmth, food, and protection. In this period of extreme dependence the infant does not distinguish itself from the external world, which is coextensive with the mother: there are no ego boundaries separating self and other and no reflective ego. The dawning awareness of the self as separate is thus connected with the child's recognition that she is distinct from the mother, who aids in the separation process by mirroring back to the child, confirming its existence, providing recognition as well as nurturance. Object-relations theorists thus stress that the self is born in relationship; separateness can only be established by a sense of relatedness to and difference from another. This ambivalent process of separation and individuation involves loss as well as gain: the child wants to be independent, yet increasing autonomy means losing the original union with the mother and abandoning the original state of oneness.

Separation and individuation are particularly complex psychological tasks for daughters, Chodorow argues, and never as fully completed as for sons. Because the mother identifies more closely with the female child (whom she is more likely to see as an extension of herself), she does not create as clear boundaries separating herself from her daughter as she does from her son. The sex differences make the male child clearly a "differentiated other" while the daughter is more easily considered part of the self. The daughter, in turn, may find it difficult to escape what Chodorow terms her "primary" sense of oneness with the being with whom she was once merged; unlike her brother, she cannot use the barrier of gender difference to establish her autonomy. (46–47)

What is useful to critics like O'Brien about this way of describing Chodorow's view of individual development? First, it explains how Chodorow establishes the existence of a separate female identity: "women tend to define themselves in relationships to others, whereas men do not." Second, it gives value to a previously neglected relationship—the relation between mother and daughter—and, at the same time, it is capable of explaining women's ambivalent feelings toward their mothers. Daughters feel connected to their mothers but also "want to be independent." Further, this way of discussing female development implicitly cuts across differences produced by race, class, or culture, which are never mentioned: all women are daughters; all mothers are women.[7]

In this relational account of female identity many feminists have found the basis for a specifically female poetics that dramatizes the fusion and separation of mother and daughter.[8] In an article by Claire Kahane, for example, the shared space of female identity becomes a space that nurtures women's writing. Kahane uses the Winnicottian concept of "potential space" (Winnicott calls it the space "between the baby and the mother") to give the relationship between mother and daughter a utopian linguistic dimension. She explains: "As Winnicott develops its parameters, it is a space of illusion where external and internal reality intersect, where, unchallenged, the subject's own discourse can fuse with an external discourse to create new meanings. This is Winnicott's area of creative play, a space necessary to the imagination. This is the space in which new meaning to categories of gender can be forged" (89). Ironically, the concept of "potential space" is actually bound up with requirements for "good enough" mothering. Winnicott repeatedly explains that only if the baby is given "sensitive management" can it use the potential space for identity formation: "In the state of confidence that grows up when a mother can do this difficult thing well (not if she is unable to do it) . . . confidence in the mother makes an intermediate playground . . . a potential space. . . ."(*Playing and Reality* 47) or "A baby can be *fed* without love, but loveless or impersonal *management* cannot succeed in producing a new autonomous human child. Here where there is trust and reliability is a potential space" (*Playing and Reality* 108). Only by ignoring the specific power relations specified by Winnicott, that is, the subordination of the mother to the child, can Kahane go on to suggest that in this "potential space" literary critics (in the role of infants?) will rediscover "the maternal voice that speaks especially to women" (90).

For Kahane, O'Brien, and many other feminists, Chodorow's object-relations account of female identity seems progressive, to allow for more specifically female forms of expression and identity than do other forms of psychoanalysis. And perhaps it *is* progressive in so far as it has encouraged women to talk about a central issue in their lives, their relation to mothering. While her way of describing motherhood may be problematic, the very fact that Chodorow broached this topic is important. Furthermore, it always feels liberating—though reversal is a somewhat static operation—to turn upside down a traditional structure of domination and submission. O'Brien, and others, describe Freud's theories as "male biased" in that these theories focus on the father's role in the oedipal stage; object-relations theorists and feminists influenced by them revalue the preoedipal stage that Chodorow casts both as feminine and as the founding determinant of female experience. Critics have found in Chodorow's work a basis for supporting a utopian myth of female relationships and even a new, preoedipal language in which to describe them. With the aid of Chodorow's paradigm, many feminist critics have breathed a sigh of relief and turned from an analysis of patriarchal oppression to an appreciation of the drama of the daughter's psychological and discursive relations with her mother.

All of the feminist critical analyses based on Chodorow's theory of mothering use it to illuminate the experience of a daughter's relationship to her mother, which is always articulated as the daughter's desire for identification and her difficulties with separation. Her struggle to achieve autonomy constitutes the daughter's bildungsroman. Even in the best of Chodorovian analyses, this psychological dynamic inevitably becomes an appeal to a referent that is natural and authentic. Linda Williams, for example, in her article "'Something Else Besides a Mother': *Stella Dallas* and the Maternal Melodrama," is self-conscious about the dangers of slipping into the language of authenticity, while, at the same time, she wants to describe a mode of representation that is specifically feminine. As Williams explains, "My argument . . . is not only that some maternal melodramas have historically addressed female audiences about issues of primary concern to women, but that these melodramas also have reading positions structured into their texts that demand female reading competence. This competence derives from the different way women take on their identities under patriarchy and is a direct result of the social fact of female mothering" (7–8).

Making use of Chodorow, Williams argues that this alternate subjectivity, based on a primary identification with the mother, allows the female viewer to resist the masochistic image of the mother offered in *Stella Dallas*. Ann Kaplan, in a reply to Williams, says that such resistance is impossible given that the female viewer is constructed by the film's mechanisms, which insist on patriarchal norms for femininity. Yet despite her objections to Williams's analysis, Kaplan still tries to preserve the "truth" of Chodorow's view of female subjectivity: "To the degree that Williams uses the Chodorow point to show that *Stella Dallas* is a text that specifically constructs multiple identifications addressed to women's needs, I agree with her" (42). Because Chodorow has developed a compelling and systematic descriptive model of female subjectivity and experience, even a skeptical critic like Kaplan (or Williams for that matter) is quite understandably reluctant to give it up.

In a review of *The (M)other Tongue: Essays in Feminist Psychoanalytic Interpretation*, Jane Gallop comments on Chodorow's remarkable influence: "Chodorow is everywhere in the book, mentioned in three-fourths of the essays and providing its theoretical framework and coherence" (319). In describing how the anthology seems both to glorify the mother and hide differences between feminists, Gallop endorses Chodorow's views about the daughter's relation to the mother. According to Gallop, feminist contributors to the anthology treat the maternal as Chodorow describes daughters treating the mother: they want to idealize and identify with the mother. Within the mother's embrace all feminists can identify with each other. Gallop argues that feminists need to go beyond identification in order to acknowledge the mother's subjectivity, her otherness. Gallop's analysis of *The (M)other Tongue* is Chodorovian, though Gallop has to work hard to make Chodorow's theory seem centrally concerned with the articulation of the mother's alterity.

Gallop's alliance with Chodorow is surprising in so far as it covers over the difference between Chodorow's "social sciences" version of psychoanalysis and Gallop's Lacanian theoretical framework. Chodorow has recently spelled out the difference between object-relations feminism and feminisms (like Gallop's) that take psychoanalysis "as story." Chodorow writes: "We [sic] are more concerned, however interpretively, with how things empirically 'are'" (*Feminism and Psychoanalytic Theory* 194). Chodorow, a trained sociologist, seems attracted to object-relations theory precisely because it conflates the symbolic and the real so that phantasmic identities such as the self become "true." Despite this difference between Chodorovian feminism and that of feminist theorists who locate the mother's otherness (indeed, subjectivity itself) in language, Gallop writes, " . . . as becomes clear in object-relations theory and particularly in Chodorow, the mother is the site of something which is both other and not quite other, of the other as self and the self as other" (317). But this confusion of self and other does not clearly emerge in Chodorow's writing. In *The Reproduction of Mothering*, Chodorow does not use the term *other*. Instead, she uses the words *object* or *not-me* and she never considers subjectivity as a linguistic construction, an essential aspect of the Lacanian concept of the "other." The "other" in Lacan marks the fundamental alienation that constitutes the subject as a signifier. The "object" in object-relations theory, as we have already shown in the first chapter, is increasingly dependent upon a belief in an independently existing reality in which the mother is "naturally" an origin who nurtures the child's self. Where is Gallop getting the language she here attributes to object-relations theory? Gallop explains in a footnote: "I owe the phrases 'other as self' and 'self as other' to a related use by Naomi Schor" (317n.8). The prestige and power of Chodorow's work in 1987, the year in which Gallop's article was published, is still so great that Gallop chooses to superimpose Lacanian theory upon Chodorow's work in order to redeem it. Gallop's linguistic maneuver disguises Chodorow's construction of feminine identity as a prediscursive creation of the mother-child relationship.

It may seem to some readers that we are being overly rigid about the distinctions between "self" and "subject" or "other" and "object." What is at stake here? The language of "self" and "object" moves us toward an empiricism that works to shore up a sense of normalcy oppressive to women; the language of "subject" and "other" acknowledges the alienating, divisive work of unconscious fantasy that is powerfully constitutive of identity. That this language has become slippery in appropriations of Chodorow's work points to the immensity of her influence, an influence that has been, at times, almost hegemonic. There is something genuinely surprising about Gallop's effort to make Lacan's work homologous with Chodorow's theory given the powerfully disruptive mode of criticism for which Gallop is known. Of course, Gallop's conflation of Lacan and Chodorow is not a problem if one wants a single, unified story of motherhood. Since it is our view that preserving distinctions—between Klein and Winnicott, between Lacan and Chodorow—helps to unfix the position of the maternal by providing alternate readings, we have resisted the desire to reconcile psychoanalytic versions of the place of the mother, though points of convergence must be acknowledged. Our point here is *not* to privilege Lacan—or to see him as pure in his difference from object-relations theory—but to bring out resources within psychoanalysis that can contest reigning claims to the *truth* of women's experience. As we have shown, the power of Chodorow's work to provide a foundational, universalist story for feminism has much to do with the conservative way Winnicott fixes the mother as an origin, a positioning that feminists have long recognized as burdensome to women. The simultaneous desire to embrace and undercut a unified account of the mother is wonderfully illustrated in Gallop's reading of Chodorow.

Because she can interpret Chodorow as a Lacanian, Gallop is able to constitute herself and Chodorow as members of a privileged group that recognizes the mother's alterity, that is, the mother as truly "other." Let us look more closely at how Gallop constructs the genealogy of this privileged group. First, Gallop credits Chodorow with initiating feminist discussion about "the blind spot of psychoanalysis": in psychoanalysis the mother is never a subject. In support of this claim, Gallop quotes Chodorow, who says in *The Reproduction of Mothering* that "male theorists . . . ignore the mother's involvements outside her relationship to her infant . . ." (87). Gallop's next move is to point out that although Chodorow apparently originates this perception of a bias against maternal subjectivity, Chodorow simply does not take her perception far enough. Susan Suleiman does this work for Chodorow. In her essay in *The (M)other Tongue*, Suleiman takes Chodorow's idea a step further, discovering a bias against the mother's subjectivity not only in the writings of the "fathers" of psychoanalysis but also in those of its "mothers"—Helene Deutsch, Melanie Klein, Alice Balint, Karen Horney. Gallop says that, here, Suleiman is "explicitly following Chodorow's lead" (324). Finally, Gallop herself goes further still, demonstrating "the bias against maternal alterity in contemporary psychoanalytic feminist criticism" (325). As an example of such bias, Gallop points to Ronnie Scharfman's literary criticism. Scharfman, according to Gallop, uncritically uses Winnicott's theory, which refuses to see the mother as the other: "Scharfman does not critique Winnicott's position but simply produces a very agile literary application of it" (325).

Gallop can criticize Scharfman's, but not Chodorow's, reliance upon Winnicott. Yet Gallop acknowledges that Scharfman's "literary application of object-relations theory . . . has come down through Chodorow" (325). Notice here that Chodorow, who Gallop claims originated the perception that psychoanalysis is blind to maternal alterity, now becomes the origin of a bias *against* maternal alterity. It is at this point that Gallop's genealogy of the growing feminist awareness of the "blind spot of psychoanalysis" reveals its own blind spot. Gallop asks Scharfman to criticize Winnicott without making it explicit that Chodorow, too, relies on his construction of the "good enough" mother and thus crucially limits her concern with maternal subjectivity. Instead of directly criticizing Chodorow, Gallop uses Chodorow to legitimate her attack on Scharfman, whose Chodorovian literary analysis, Gallop paradoxically claims, does not take into account maternal subjectivity. The incoherence of Gallop's position suggests both the tenaciousness of Chodorow's paradigm of female identity and its increasing vulnerability to questions about how object-relations theory, and certainly psychoanalysis itself, frames the mother.

As Gallop notices, some feminists have acknowledged the erasure of the mother's subjectivity in psychoanalytic theory, while other feminist writers have continued to emphasize the daughter's story at the expense of the mother's. Marianne Hirsch's *The Mother/ Daughter Plot: Narrative, Psychoanalysis, Feminism* tries to be fair to both mothers and daughters. In describing the writing of her book, Hirsch says that Nancy Chodorow's *Reproduction of Mothering* initially inspired her to write a book focusing "on *daughters* rather than *mothers*, on female development as the daughter's process of apprenticeship to the mother" (19). Yet, says Hirsch, she became increasingly aware that maternal experience appeared "external to our operative paradigms which were focused almost entirely on the perspective of the child" (23). In her book, she tries to find a new framework that will allow her to tell the mother's story. She turns to literature, especially literature by African-American women writers, to show how the mother's voice might be articulated. As Hirsch's book progresses, it shows a more and more explicit "dissatisfaction with its own (Chodorovian) framework and [the search] for another framework" that will take into account maternal subjectivity (174–75). Much more directly than Gallop, Hirsch questions Chodorow and seems anxious to go beyond her paradigm.

In response to the psychoanalytic focus on the child, Hirsch asks, "What model or definition of subjectivity might be derived from a theory that begins with mothers rather than with children?" (197). What would the voice of maternal subjectivity sound like? In light of Hirsch's explicit desire to listen to the multiplicity of maternal experiences derived from differences in race, class, and culture, her answer seems surprisingly reductive: the mother's subjectivity is defined solely through her anger. "To be angry . . . is to create a space of separation, to isolate oneself temporarily; such breaks in connection, such disruptions of relationship again challenge the role that not only psychoanalysis, but also culture itself assigns to mothers" (170).

According to Hirsch, maternal anger can take two forms: anger on behalf of the child (which is Clytemnestra's anger) or anger directed toward the husband that turns into violence against the children (which is Medea's anger).[9] Of these two forms of maternal anger, Hirsch focuses primarily on the first. She writes more convincingly about Alice Walker's essay, "One Child of One's Own: A Meaningful Digression within the Work(s)," in which Walker aligns herself with her daughter and turns her anger outward, than she does about the work of Toni Morrison, whose novel *Beloved* is about a mother who kills her daughter (anger against her racist society is here transformed into violence against her daughter, thus requiring an analysis of culture rather than simply of feminine psychology). Hirsch's emphasis on maternal subjectivity as anger on behalf of the child is finally embedded in a notion of maternal caretaking that hardly departs from the object-relations model. Once again the requirements for subjectivity are oppressively formulated in accordance with the child's imagined needs.[10] As in Chodorow's work, these needs are assumed to be real, rather than described as constructions that might themselves be shaped by a dynamic defined and required by object-relations theory. As a result, even as Hirsch discusses maternal anger and subjectivity in Alice Walker's essays and stories, she anxiously returns to a discussion of the daughter's subjectivity, as though that subjectivity somehow exists in pure opposition to the mother's. Underlying this compulsion is a basically problematic conception of the constitution of identity. In Hirsch's revision of Winnicott and Chodorow, feminine identity is constituted in a dynamic between a self (daughter or mother), and a selfless mirror (daughter or mother). What has happened to social context, to male desire and power?

Hirsch is aware that a feminist family romance informs Chodorow's work. Indeed one of the valuable features of Hirsch's compelling book is its placement of Chodorow within a historical context. Hirsch writes that in the 1970s feminists turned to psychoanalysis as "the instrument of a vision of difference, of a model of female subject-formation and of female specificity that might redefine" denigrating images of women's relationships (131). She sees that Chodorow, and other feminists, downplay the importance of men to show the "benefits and limits of same-sex bonding" (133). Despite her awareness of this feminist family romance, Hirsch is finally not willing to give up Chodorow's paradigm of female subject-formation, despite its limitations, because it seems to offer a key to authentic female experience.[11] When Hirsch talks about experience she sometimes places it in italics for emphasis, while at other times she places the word in quotation marks—e.g., "Theory covers over 'experience'" (171). How does theory cover over experience, if experience is not a bedrock, or to put it delicately, a "bedrock"? Our point is simply that experience is always framed (or, as Hirsch herself would say, "plotted") and that Hirsch's focus on founding paradigms of female experience (Electra/Demeter/Clytemnestra) as mother-daughter stories is a familiar framework of Chodorovian criticism with its tales of female development, mothers and daughters. Hirsch operates within this frame despite her desire to transcend the limits of psychoanalysis so that she can represent the mother's story. Paradoxically, the more Hirsch focuses on the mother's story, in rapid oscillation with the daughter's story, the more she neglects larger frames that she knows are important: race, class, patriarchal culture.

In our analysis of Winnicott we showed how object-relations theory develops a language of the real self. Chodorow, following in this tradition, similarly develops a notion of a "core" female identity. The discourse that tells us the truth about experience often slips from analysis into the language of prescription. Interestingly, Marianne Hirsch ends her book with a long paragraph listing what feminist fictions and theories should do.

> Such fictions, such theories, will have to be grounded in the material and repetitive work of mothers in culture even as they account for the structures of language and representation. They will have to build the most sophisticated models of individual and group relations to language and will have to affirm a necessary polyvocality, even as they reorganize the political power women can derive from speaking, and from speaking with one voice. They will have to account for women's and for mothers' collusion with patriarchy even as they imagine ways of overcoming that collusion. Such fictions, such theories, will

have to be supple enough to respect and reflect the vast difference among mothers who mother in vastly different social and cultural conditions. Such theories will have to relinquish the exclusive dependence on psychoanalytic models and will have to integrate psychoanalysis with other perspectives—historical, social, economic. They will have to refuse the split between theory and practice and will have to integrate the perspectives of those who fight for better policies with those who invent better theories; they will have to respond to the practical needs of women's, men's, and children's lives. They will have to include aggression, ambivalence, contradiction, even as they wish for connection, support, and affiliation. They will have to include the body even as they avoid essentialism. They will have to imagine ways that, in spite of repeated conflicts and disappointments, women and men can parent together, and ways for women and men to parent alone. And they will have to oppose, as rigorously as possible, mystifications of maternity and femininity, by creating ways to theorize adult, maternal as well as paternal, experience and by transcending the limited perspective of the developing child. (199)

This oppressive list of imperatives, directed to what certainly is an audience largely consisting of women, sets up an impossible task. The expectation that a "good enough" feminism could meet such a contradictory set of demands recalls Winnicott's radio broadcasts and their contradictory expectations for "good enough" mothers.

Rather than compulsively trying to do it all, we have chosen to ask how the conjuncture of object relations and feminism has naturalized such demands, demands that continue to position us as insatiable children and selfless mothers. We are not arguing that these unconscious identifications have no validity, but rather that when functioning as universal referents, these positions drastically constrain the possibilities of feminist cultural analysis by insistently linking women to a maternal role that is defined as primary. Indeed, in *The Reproduction of Mothering* the mother, finally, originates stereotypes of masculinity and femininity. Chodorow, of course, appropriated the mother-child dyad of object-relations theory in the name of a feminist critique of the sexual division of labor, though the object-relations account of psychological development always turns patriarchal culture into a secondary formation. Still, Chodorow begins from the position of a feminist trying to understand the oppression of women. As we shift from Chodorow's exploration of mothering and feminine identity in order to scrutinize the work of Julia Kristeva, we largely leave feminism behind, while object-relations theory remains with us. Kristeva uses object-relations theory to describe the psychotic underside of the Symbolic as a dark continent of women.

Chapter 3

Kristeva's Death-Bearing Mother

On the cover of Julia Kristeva's *Black Sun: Depression and Melancholia* is a detail from a painting by Hans Holbein the Younger, "Portrait of the Artist's Wife, Elizabeth Binzenstock, and Her Two Children, Philip and Catherine." The detail depicts Philip's head, framed in darkness, his eyes gazing solemnly, perhaps dejectedly, at an object that exists beyond the edge of the picture. Kristeva's book, *Black Sun*, seems to refer to this son, whose gaze is ever torn from a lost object, an object that Kristeva's text will suggest is the mother: "The child king becomes irredeemably sad before uttering his first words; this is because he has been irrevocably, desperately separated from the mother, a loss that causes him to try to find her again, along with other objects of love, first in the imagination and then in words" (6). Unlike the detail on the jacket cover of *Black Sun*, Holbein's complete painting tells a different story. Philip's mother is not absent from Holbein's painting; she is the dominant figure. Her face with its expression of inexpressible weariness seems to provide a comment on the title of the painting: "The *Artist's* Wife . . . and *Her* Two Children" (our emphasis). The painting thus provokes questions about the dichotomous relation between "artist" and "wife," father and mother, owner and property. And Philip's gaze is ambiguous rather than clearly focused on his mother. His field of vision includes both his mother and his baby sister Catherine. The Holbein painting, then, complicates the story Kristeva wants to tell about the mourned object. Like the cover of *Black Sun*, Kristeva's text artfully frames the child so as to privilege the son and the father/artist while transforming the mother and daughter into phantoms. This kind of framing is not a feminist one. Kristeva's reductive emphasis on the (male) child has its origin in psychoanalysis.

There is no simple way to specify the various psychoanalytic discourses that are crucial to Julia Kristeva's account of the mother. In the last chapter, we pointed out that Chodorow opposes object-relations theory to forms of psychoanalysis that insist on the role of language in the formation of the subject ("we [*sic*] are more concerned . . . with how things empirically 'are'" [Chodorow, *Feminism and Psychoanalytic Theory* 194]). In contrast, Kristeva's work seems to link a Lacanian account of identity and language acquisition with a transgressive focus on the mother (and on the child's fantasy of the mother). Kristeva's turn toward a discussion of the maternal has typically been lauded as a masterful feminist subversion of Lacan. Cynthia Chase writes, for example, that Kristeva powerfully interrogates Lacan so as to allow a place for maternal desire *and* the child's vacillating reading of the mother as both imaginary father and abject mother, a mother whose desire may not signify.[1] We will talk more about what Kristeva is here contributing, but for the moment it seems important to contextualize these contributions as Chase does not—as indeed no one has done. Kristeva's analysis of maternal desire and the child's trouble as interpreter is more indebted to object-relations theory, specifically to the work of André Green, than has been previously acknowledged. Many feminist readings of Kristeva's work have lent it a false coherence that has led to a misreading of Kristeva's politics, of, so to speak, "where she is coming from." Far from offering a feminist subversion of the language of Lacan, Kristeva's most recent discussion of the mother in *Black Sun* emphasizes the pathology of nonphallic maternal desire and the child's fantasized interpretations of it.

Lacan conceives of psychic life as like language, as a chain of signifiers severed from external referents. He narrates the story of the child's entry into the symbolic order as a transition that involves loss and splitting. In the mirror stage, the child's subjectivity and desire depend on its separation both from itself (it discovers itself in an image or signifier) and from the mother.[2] According to Lacan, the symbolic order in which the "I" is constituted must be paternal. As Jacqueline Rose explains: "The phallus . . . breaks the two term relation and initiates the order of exchange. . . . Castration means first of all this—that the child's desire for the mother does not refer *to* her but *beyond* her, to an object, the phallus, whose status is first imaginary (the object presumed to satisfy her desire) and then symbolic (the recognition that desire cannot be satisfied)" (*Feminine Sexuality*

38). In the castration complex, the child finds its exclusive desire for the mother prohibited by a third term, the father (or paternal metaphor), who is encountered in the mother's desire for something that is outside her relation with the child. Without the intervention of this third term that breaks up the asocial mother-child dyad, the child cannot come into existence as a subject and cannot participate with pleasure and vitality in the symbolic order. In this account, the symbolic order can be understood as a compensation for the loss of a relatively unmediated relation to the mother. According to this logic, a refusal of the father's crucial function as agent of the symbolic order can only lead to psychic and linguistic difficulties.

Julia Kristeva's *Black Sun* is concerned with depression and melancholia, and especially with a symptom of those illnesses that she calls "asymbolia" (9). Asymbolia, an inability to use language to compensate for the lost object, results from a subject's refusal to give up an archaic attachment to the maternal object. Kristeva vividly describes the deadly effects of a captivation with what she calls the "Thing." Using Lacanian terms, she describes the "Thing" as "the real that does not lend itself to signification" (13). As her argument evolves, the relation to the mother is substituted for the relation to the "Thing." For example, in a section of *Black Sun* entitled "Death-Bearing Woman," the failure to commit *matricide* is what creates the symptoms of depression, one of which is the death of speech (asymbolia).

> For a man and for a woman the loss of the mother is a biological and psychic necessity, the first step on the way to becoming autonomous. Matricide is our vital necessity, the sine-qua-non of our individuation, provided that it takes place under optimal circumstances and can be eroticized—whether the lost object is recovered as erotic object (as is the case for male heterosexuality or female homosexuality), or it is transposed by means of an unbelievable symbolic effort, the advent of which one can only admire, which eroticizes the *other* (the other sex, in the case of the heterosexual woman) or transforms cultural constructs into a "sublime" erotic object . . . . The lesser or greater violence of the matricidal drive . . . entails when it is hindered, its inversion on the self; the maternal object having been introjected, the depressive or melancholic putting to death of the self is what follows,

instead of matricide. . . . In order to protect mother I kill myself
while knowing—phantasmic and protective knowledge—that it
comes from her, the death-bearing she Ge-henna. . . . Thus my
hatred is safe and my matricidal guilt erased. . . .

For a woman, whose specular identification with the mother
as well as the introjection of the maternal body and self are more
immediate, such an inversion of matricidal drive into a death-
bearing maternal image is more difficult, if not impossible. Indeed, how can She be that bloodthirsty Fury, since I am She
(sexually and narcissistically), She is I? Consequently the hatred
I bear her is not oriented toward the outside but is locked within
myself. There is no hatred, only an implosive mood that walls
itself in and kills me secretly, very slowly. . . . Modest, silent,
without verbal or desiring bonds with others, she wastes away
by striking moral and physic blows against herself, which, never-
theless, do not give her sufficient pleasures. Until the fatal
blow—the definitive nuptials of the Dead Woman with the
Same, whom she did not kill. (27–30)

One hears in this passage Lacan's emphasis on the necessity of break-
ing up the mother-child dyad, but there are new elements added to
his story of subject formation. Kristeva discusses a matricidal drive,
denials of that drive, encrypted death-bearing maternal images, femininity both as an impediment to individuation and an encounter with
death and silence. These elaborations of Lacan's thesis, with their
new emphasis on the maternal, owe a debt to the French psychoanalyst André Green, and to object-relations theory.[3]

Green's work is made explicitly present in *Black Sun* through
Kristeva's references to his *Narcissisme de vie, Narcissisme de mort* and
to his notions of negative narcissism and the "psychic void." In addition, there are other areas of coincidence between Green's work and
Kristeva's that are not explicitly mentioned. Green, for example,
shares Kristeva's interest in psychoses, the maternal, and in affect
(particularly its potential as language). Indeed, by looking at Green's
work it is possible to understand more clearly Kristeva's departures
from Lacan and her attachment to object-relations theory.

Green, while influenced by Lacan, argues that Lacan does not
pay enough attention to either psychosis or affect. "It is sad . . . to
see the how the theory advanced by the most original author in

French psychoanalysis only contributes ideas which suggest that, with psychotics, all that the analyst can do is establish the fact of the foreclosure of the paternal metaphor" (Green 237). For Green, the Lacanian emphasis on language precludes significant analysis of the situation of psychotics and borderline patients whose problems seem to be linked to a space before language where the vicissitudes of the passions are inscribed. According to Green, studies of the psychotic draw the analyst's attention to the preoedipal period and the process of the self in formation, to a realm in which failures of maternal care become a crucial concern. In Green's view, "descriptions of the mother-infant relationship have not been taken far enough" (244). Not surprisingly, Green describes himself as indebted to writers of the British School, otherwise known as the school of object-relations.

A chapter from Green's *Narcissisme de vie, Narcissisme de mort*, written in 1980, provides a paradigm for understanding problems associated with mourning for the lost object, a paradigm that Kristeva will draw upon in *Black Sun*. In this chapter, entitled "The Dead Mother," Green explains that Freud and French psychoanalysts influenced by Lacan have concentrated upon the importance of the "dead father" and in doing so centralized the importance of castration, "castrasizing" other anxieties (145).[4] In contrast, Klein and her followers have elevated the maternal object (the breast) and anxieties relating to its loss, that is, depressive anxieties. Whereas Freud, according to Green, never considered the effects of bad mothering, Klein at least gave play to the idea of the bad internal object: the "bad mother" who is the phantasized production of the infant's projections. Klein, however, rarely discussed the actual mother; it would be left for Winnicott to speak about mothers as agents. Green follows Winnicott by considering the psychic consequences for the child of a real event upon an actual mother. Though both Winnicott and Green discuss the mother as an origin, Winnicott is primarily concerned with articulating the attributes of "good enough" mothering; Green is primarily concerned with describing the effects of bad mothering. Green also mildly rebukes Winnicott's lack of interest in the father's role and in the child's sexuality. Attempting a synthesis of psychoanalytic theories of loss, Green discusses the ramifications of what he calls "the dead mother complex" upon the child's understanding of the primal scene and, eventually, the Oedipus complex.

According to Green, the "dead mother complex" reveals itself in the child's depression: "the essential characteristic of this depression is that it takes place in the presence of the object, which is itself absorbed by a bereavement" (149). In other words, the mother is not actually dead; she is self-absorbed as a result of a loss. The child experiences her absorption as a catastrophe, as a narcissistic wound. In place of positive primary narcissism, which Green characterizes as "tending towards unity and identity," the child develops negative primary narcissism that is connected with feelings of emptiness. The "dead" object thus draws the child toward a "deathly, deserted universe" (167). The "dead mother complex" informs all later stages of development. For instance, in the primal scene, an important determinant of the Oedipus complex, the child feels incapable of competing against a rival who more successfully awakens the dead mother, "animating her, rendering life to her" (159). The victim of the "dead mother complex" compensates for this added narcissistic wound in a number of ways, including turning to the compensations of intense intellectual activity and artistic creation (160). Green's account makes it clear that the "dead" mother is not dead enough. Indeed, she has enormous, if not monstrous power.

Initially it would appear that the "dead mother complex" arises not so much from the mother's activities as her passivity. Indeed, it is because her active interest in the child has been suddenly replaced by a new, passive disinterest that the child becomes concerned to imprison the mother by whom he feels abandoned. The child takes measures to "bury her alive" so that she remains in the child's psyche as a "cold core" (150), a "black" void (146) associated with mourning. But there is a subtle shift in Green's description of the mother at this point. The inhabitant of this tomb, the fantasized dead mother, actively encourages the child's captivity in order to compensate herself for her own loss. The child "remains prisoner to her economy of survival. He thinks he has got rid of his dead mother. In fact, she only leaves him in peace in the measure that she herself is left in peace. As long as there is no candidate to the succession, she can well let her child survive, certain to be the only one to possess this inaccessible love" (156). In this way, the fantasized mother maliciously capitalizes on opportunities for self-promotion provided by her own entombment. In the child's fantasy, she is now an actively hostile force. Using military metaphors, Green explains that the analyst's treatment of the depressed patient involves waging a battle against the dead mother.

> Very often the analyst says to himself: "This time it's done, the old woman is really dead, he (or she) will finally be able to live and I shall be able to breathe a little." Then a small traumatism appears in the transference or in life which gives the maternal imago renewed vitality, if I may put it this way. It is because she is a thousand-headed hydra whom one believes one has beheaded with each blow; whereas in fact only one of its heads has been struck off. Where then is the beast's neck? (158)

At this point, the analyst (and Green) is identifying with what Green has described as the patient's fantasy and seems to have lost sight entirely of the actual mother who is simply in mourning. Though Green has criticized Klein for her neglect of the "maternal variable," Green himself seems locked into a funhouse constituted by threatening, all-too-active maternal imagos. In Green's text, the mother becomes the "vampire" (164), the "hydra" (158), and "the beast" (158), the monstrous ruler of a "dark empire" (198). (Kristeva shares Green's reliance upon military metaphors to describe the infant's separation from the mother, though certainly Kristeva's language is not as virulent as Green's. For example, she says in "Place Names" that the child's acquisition of language is achieved by means of "a victorious confrontation [with the mother], never finished with her" [*Desire in Language* 291].)

When the mother is "good enough," she, apparently, also becomes a dead maternal object, but one that dies in a less threatening way. Her death "must be slow and gentle so that the memory of her love does not perish, but may nourish the love that she will generously offer to her who takes her place" (172). Green assumes that the lost object will be replaced by another female object, a genealogy of women as reassuring supports for the (male?) ego. Through her "effacement," the mother is transformed into a framing structure or "receptacle," a potential space for the ego and its object representations.[5] Green's "good enough" mother is obviously much like Winnicott's mother who "holds" the child (a connection Green himself makes in his essay). For Green, however, this maternal holding makes possible representations infused with vital affects—both love and hate. In the "dead mother complex," the ego lacks a solid framework and object representations lack "vital character" (166). While searching for lost meaning, victims of the "dead mother complex" prove themselves gifted at representation and interpretation, but these representations are finally disconnected from emotions.

For the Greenian analyst, then, it is more important to read affects than words. Indeed, affects constitute a language that is "older than speech" (199). (In *Black Sun*, Kristeva says much the same thing: " . . . affect is the most archaic inscription of inner and outer events" [23].) Affective language is older than speech because it is connected to the biological energies and the passions that are the "matrix of symbolization" (Green 251). For Green and Kristeva, affect exists at the border between the maternal unnameable and the paternal Symbolic. Both theorists are interested in psychosis because it seems to provide access to this archaic and unexplored realm. (However, they distinguish the situation of depressive from that of psychotic on the basis of the fragile relation the depressive maintains with a paternal signifier: the depressive uses signs though these signs are separated from affects.) In *Black Sun*, Julia Kristeva explains that "sadness leads us into the enigmatic realm of *affects* . . . very rudimentary representation, presign and prelanguage" (21). Psychotics are those who, "for want of losing the mother" (53), deny the "father's function, which is precisely to guarantee the establishment of the signifier" (45). What Chase interpreted as Kristeva's progressive opening up of maternal desire as fruitfully unsignifiable is bleakly fixed for Kristeva in *Black Sun;* if the mother's desire does not signify to the infant a desire for the phallus, the infant is doomed to suffer. As Green puts it: "There are mothers who want to wipe out any trace of the father in the child. And we know the result: a psychotic structure" (295). Kristeva's case histories, as we shall see, make much the same point.

Kristeva's analysis of depression and melancholia in *Black Sun*, and her preoccupation with death and the resurrection of the dead mother, reveals her indebtedness to Green's "The Dead Mother." Kristeva's uncritical use of Green is surprising given her earlier attentiveness to maternal subjectivity. Green never questions for a moment the Winnicottian assumption that the mother should be in service to the infant, thus the mother's sense of loss, interpreted by

Green as an empirical moment of bereavement, is always, even if implicitly, a failure of sorts, rather than a problem of the social structuring of woman's position. If, on the other hand, we understand the mother's position of powerlessness in patriarchy, then the woman, especially in her position as mother, could be seen as responding, at this moment, to the imbalance of power within patriarchy as an experience of loss. Kristeva, in both her articles "Place Names" and "Stabat Mater," considers the mother's desire, her subjectivity as actively creating a dialectic (the transference) with the infant. In "Place Names" (1977), for example, just as the mother "analyzes" the child, the child "analyzes" the mother, which simply means that he [sic] serves to release "her anguish," even her fury. This anguish is the result of her realization of loss—of power but also of her child, whom she wants to keep locked within a delicious symbiosis with her. Thus Kristeva acknowledges the mother's frustration rather than simply the baby's at the moment when "good enough" mothering or "optimal frustration of the baby" is required for the infant to enter the Symbolic. Kristeva shows the devastating demands upon the woman required to be the "good enough" mother—she must, Kristeva tells us, either acknowledge her castration or become hysterical. Unfortunately, in *Black Sun*, Kristeva seems to lose sight of this difficulty for the mother entirely when she presents the mother's service to the male infant as so inevitable as to appear natural.

The mother's role is naturalized when she becomes the origin of sexual difference rather than a casualty of existing structures of sexual difference. Like Chodorow, Kristeva "genders" an apparently neutral system of interpretation. That is, she accepts, as does Chodorow, (though without even the hint of skepticism that we get in Chodorow) the requirements of child development described by an object-relations theorist and then proceeds to point out the different ramifications of this requirement for infant boys and girls. Specifically, Green's article, "The Dead Mother," contains little discussion of the different problems men and women might have with separation from the maternal object. Yet this difference is an important question for Kristeva, who asserts that while "matricide is a vital necessity" for the psychic health of both men and women, women find it enormously difficult to murder the mother. They remain enthralled by the "Thing," suffering from what is obviously the "dead mother complex," though Kristeva prefers the more general description, "melancholy/depressive" composite (*Black Sun* 10). Because women identify with the mother that they have encrypted within themselves, they too feel dead. We are a long way from Chodorow's more benign view of mother-daughter relationships. Yet both Chodorow and Kristeva preserve conventional gender identities. While Chodorow can dwell upon the mother's success as a nurturer, an identity we might not mind, Kristeva dwells upon the mother's failures. In *Black Sun*, she attempts to provide both theoretical and clinical evidence that the mother-daughter relation is pathogenic. This "truth" is demonstrated by case histories of depressed women drawn from her clinical practice. "Being caught in woman's speech is not merely a matter of chance that could be explained by the greater frequency of feminine depressions—a sociologically proven fact. This may also reveal an aspect of feminine sexuality: its addiction to the maternal Thing and its lesser aptitude for restorative perversion" (71). Women are more sick than men.

Kristeva thinks she is gendering Green's account, but that account is not neutral to begin with. Green believes women *are* more sick than men and that this sickness is an intrinsic feature of femininity. In his article "Aggression, Femininity, Paranoia, and Reality" (1971), reprinted in *On Private Madness*, Green expands on Freud's concept of femininity, adding to it the concept of feminine paranoia as part of the "normal" condition of female sexuality. According to Green, a woman's paranoia undoes her primary identification with the mother; paranoid delusion is a refusal to identify with the mother except as an alienating identification. Furthermore, Green is perhaps even more insistent than was Freud on the importance of female anatomy to psychic development: "We have placed some importance on *anatomical* considerations in this study. These are rarely taken into account in psychoanalysis. . . . In dealing with the dissolution of the Oedipus complex, Freud, paraphrasing Napoleon, recalls that *anatomy is destiny*. We now find with sexual destiny a *sexual reality* alongside internal and external reality. . . . It remains true that even if surgical miracles may change a person's sex, it is impossible to change his sexual destiny" (113; Green's italics). Specifically, Green argues that since the internal location of a woman's genitals is linked to the internal orientation of aggression, a woman naturally transforms destructive drives into masochism or to the delusion of being attacked from the outside, especially by a damaging penis (a projected power). This displacement of aggression onto the father, however, makes the work of mourning—of separating from the mother—difficult for the girl since the resolution of her mourning requires an erotic cathexis to a heterosexual object.

Kristeva seems to agree with Green's assumption that there are anatomically specific psychic structures. In "Stabat Mater" (1977), for example, she claims we must acknowledge "what is irreducible," that is, the "irreconcilable interest of both sexes in asserting their differences [and] the quest of each one—and of women, after all—for an appropriate fulfillment" (184). She argues that female difference reveals itself in the specific form female paranoia takes. In delineating her argument, Kristeva assimilates Green's view of feminine paranoia, and his assumptions about the nature of feminine sexuality. In her well-known essay, Kristeva attempts to explain in psychological terms how representations of the Virgin Mary have evolved. Why has the cult of the Virgin been so powerfully gratifying (despite its oppressiveness) for both women and men? Her explanation of the cult's compensations for women rests upon the assumption of the reality of feminine paranoia and the need to give it some form of expression. "The Virginal maternal is a . . . way of dealing with feminine paranoia" ("Stabat Mater" 180). Kristeva summarizes how this happens: the virginal maternal allows a "feminine denial of the other sex" through a third person, God (180); it assumes a "paranoid lust for power" by changing a woman into a queen and yet also allows her to deny her power by kneeling at the foot of her son (180); the Virgin "obstructs the desire for murder" by a "valorization of pain" (the sob) (180–81); the Virgin "assumes the paranoid fantasy of being excluded from time and death through . . . the representation of . . . the Assumption" (181); the Virgin also repudiates "the other woman" (the woman's mother) by suggesting "the image of A Unique Woman" (181). According to Kristeva, the cult of the Virgin thus allows women to satisfy the needs of feminine paranoia—especially the need to disguise a homosexual identification with the mother—while simultaneously submitting to the paternal agency of the Symbolic.

Kristeva argues that today the myth of the virgin mother has lost its power but has not yet been replaced by a myth with equivalent compensatory power. We need, she says, a new myth that will take into account the role of the maternal in feminine psychology. In "Stabat Mater" Kristeva suggests that a new language and subjectivity may emerge that remains closer to the maternal body, its experiences and psychology. While "Stabat Mater" seems to celebrate such a development, "Women's Time," written two years later (1979), reveals Kristeva's concern that the feminine attachment to the archaic maternal object may "result in paranoid types of counter-investment in the initially denied symbolic order" (201). She asserts that women (especially feminists) are increasingly involved in terrorism, a mode of activity that allows them to counterinvest the violence they have endured in the name of "fantasy of archaic fulfillment" (204). By the time *Black Sun* (1987) is published, Kristeva is arguing that without the solutions offered by Freudian and Christian orthodoxy, especially their linking of the woman to a paternal third term, women must increasingly suffer their mad (in both the senses of this term) relation to the Symbolic. In all these texts, Kristeva assumes the existence of a specifically feminine illness that has its basis in a relation to the mother, but in "Stabat Mater"—and to a lesser extent in "Women's Time"—this relation is given some revolutionary potential. In *Black Sun*, women leave the revolution and collapse into depression.

Employing a strategy of looking at women that recalls Winnicott's portrait gallery, Kristeva presents several "Illustrations of Feminine Depression." It is in this part of *Black Sun* that her unquestioning assimilation of Winnicottian object-relations theory is the strongest, perhaps because her diagnosis of her patients depends so much on Green's work. Her first portrait depicts a depressed woman, "Anne," who displays the classic symptoms of the "dead mother complex": "the patient effected a true swallowing of the hated maternal object thus preserved deep within herself and changed into a source of rage against herself and of a feeling of inner emptiness" (56). Anne's "devitalized" speech conceals affective meaning, imprisoned by the Thing, that analysis will help to release. Whereas Green has declared that the analyst and the setting "are the mother," Kristeva refuses to set up the mother alone as the object of the patient's identifications (68). In her earlier work, "Freud and Love," Kristeva writes about the position of the analyst: " . . The analyst situates himself [*sic*] on a ridge where, on the one hand, the 'maternal' position—gratifying needs, 'holding' (Winnicott)—and on the other the 'paternal' position—the differentiation, distance and prohibition that produces both meaning and absurdity—are intermingled and severed, infinitely and without end" (246). She adds that this capacity to make use of identification is "more important precisely when the patient has difficulty in establishing, or fails to establish, an object relation" (246). Since Kristeva argues in *Black Sun* that it is precisely a "dedication to the lost mother" (24) that has impeded the depressive's identification with a third party ("father, form, schema," [23]), she, not surprisingly, adopts an interventionist "paternal" position in relation to Anne by actively, even violently, manipulating and interpreting Anne's words. Indeed *Black Sun* is at least partially constructed to defend an analytic practice that privileges interpretive discourse as a counterdepressant at a time when biochemical antidepressants are ever more potent. Even when she discusses literature in later chapters of *Black Sun*, Kristeva is still demonstrating what she considers good clinical practice. Dostoyevsky's aesthetic of forgiveness, for example, is also her recommended therapeutic strategy. The analyst, she says, listens truly, tactfully, "with the utmost empathy," to the "devitalized vulgarized words," of the patient, cutting up these words to "get in touch with the other through syllables, fragments . . . , banking on what is there in order to give the depressed patient . . . a new start" (189). This is also the role of the loving "father of individual prehistory," a figure Kristeva borrows from Freud and whose characteristics she elaborates upon in her article "Freud and Love." The "father of individual prehistory" incorporates characteristics of Winnicott's and Green's analyst as the holding mother, but he also enables language. The analyst, like the loving father, allows a narcissistic regression that is not deadly because it is contained within history and speech.

In her case histories, Kristeva claims that her discursive analytic strategy is successful: Anne finally expels the dead mother. Recounting one of her dreams, Anne says: "And now here I am giving birth [to my mother] and it is she who lives again . . ." (58). For Kristeva, the trajectory of female development moves from an imprisonment by the maternal Thing to a liberating pregnancy that revitalizes the Dead Mother so that the daughter is no longer keeper of her tomb. The story of Anne thus works to confirm Kristeva's assumption that for women the relation to a primary maternal object is particularly dangerous and an identification with a paternal object is particularly beneficial.

The next illustration, a portrait of "Helen," again depicts a patient with the classic symptoms of the "dead mother complex."

Helen's mother is self-absorbed ("inhuman, artificial, nymphoma-
niac, incapable of any feeling" [74]) and Helen's oral assimilation of
her mother not only makes her feel dead but locks up her sexuality.
Frigidity, claims Kristeva, "betrays an imaginary capture by the frigid
woman of a maternal figure" (77). The frigid woman's rescue requires
the intervention of a figure that Kristeva calls a "godsend" ("Freud
and Love" 257); the godsend is comparable to Freud's "father of
individual prehistory" or Lacan's (and Green's) "third term." This
father is "more than a mother" yet "he is not a phallic mother but
rather a restoration of the mother by means of a phallic violence that
destroys the bad but also bestows and honors" (*Black Sun* 79).

Implicitly, Kristeva is differentiating her theory of depression
from Klein's, though Klein's theory is crucial to Kristeva's understanding both of primitive moments of splitting and of the death
drive as a regressive movement linked to affect, especially to the fear
of annihilation. Klein, however, did not provide a specific place for
the father as an "idealizing agency" ("Freud and Love" 261) who
makes possible primary identification and establishes the conditions
for both imagination and sublimation. (As we discussed earlier, it is
difficult to discern how the Kleinian infant would come to modify its
practices of projection, introjection, and splitting and so both enter
and resolve the depressive position.) Kristeva, then, restores the
father as a savior, though she is careful to mitigate his power: the
"father of individual prehistory" is not the stern, oedipal father and
is associated with the mother's desire (understood as desire for the
phallus).[6] This new and improved father does not prove especially
liberatory for women. The father of individual prehistory is said to
enable a woman's "triumph over the death-bearing mother," a locu-
tion that strongly enforces stereotypical sexual differences (*Black Sun*
79). Since this "triumph" involves transforming the woman's for-
merly dead interior into a source of "biological life, child-bearing, and
motherhood," femininity is rescued—by the imaginary father or by
Kristeva as analyst—so that it can be confined to its usual reproductive destiny (79).

While all of Kristeva's case histories involve women with successful professional lives, Kristeva makes true achievement and happiness synonymous with childbearing (metaphorical or literal).
Women are emphatically described in terms of their relation to their
mothers, who are blamed for their problems. Even when it would

make sense to locate a man as the source of a woman's problems, Kristeva blames the mother, reminding us, too, that the "dead mother complex" is linked to prescriptions for actual maternal behavior, rather than simply to the infant's phantasy life. This aspect of Kristeva's analysis becomes clear in her depiction of the case of "Marie-Ange." Marie-Ange's husband is unfaithful, but Kristeva explains that her patient's depression is not caused by her husband's infidelity. On the contrary, Marie-Ange has *chosen* this sort of man precisely because he reminds her of her mother, who was also unfaithful to her. In a passage called "Don Juan's Wife—Sorrowful or Terrorist," Kristeva explains that "Don Juan" vicariously satisfies her patient's erotomania for other women and so "provide[s] her with an antidepressive" (84).[7] In other words, Marie-Ange ought to be grateful to her Don Juan, especially because depressive women at the mercy of the dead mother—and without outlets for their desire—can be dangerous: "If the sexual desire underlying that passion were repressed, murder might take the place of embrace and the depressed woman might change into a terrorist" (84). The proof? "Many stories involving harems and other feminine jealousies have established the image of the poisoner as a privileged image of feminine Satanism" (85). Winnicott's view of the bad mother seems benign compared to Kristeva's way of blaming women for every oppressive position they find themselves in: as inhabitants of the harem, as wives of Don Juans, as depressives, and, finally, as single parents.

Kristeva's views about single mothers are first articulated in "Women's Time" where she claims that one of the "extreme" forms that women's rejection of the Symbolic takes is " the refusal of the paternal function by lesbian and single mothers" (205). Such choices, she claims, "cannot help but trouble an entire legal and moral order without, however, proposing an alternative to it" (205). Here she assumes that lesbians and single mothers are at once middle-class women with a wealth of "choices" and at the same time lawless terrorists motivated by regressive psychic states. In *Black Sun's* last "illustration" (scathingly labeled "Black hole" and "Virgin Mother"), Kristeva makes this point again through her depiction of her patient "Isabel," whose actions are explained as deluded and narcissistic (she desires to be both father and mother long after the cult of the Virgin has ceased to validate such feminine visions of grandeur). Yet while Kristeva both scolds lesbian and single mothers for refusing the paternal law and also defines them as "sick," it is she who refuses alternatives to her own conservative psychoanalysis. Is the heterosexual couple (even understood as phantasmic—the mother as primal object; the father as "father of individual prehistory") a necessary basis of psychic development? Is it the condition of signification? And what about cultural possibilities for restaging motherhood and its relation to sexual desire? Kristeva never asks these questions. They fall outside the frame of her analysis, which normalizes compulsory motherhood and positions language not only as paternal, but as best utilized by men, especially when language is informed by a "regressive" relation to an archaic maternal object.

Rather than repeat the efforts of other feminists to define Kristevan concepts such as the semiotic or the chora (earlier ways in which Kristeva has defined maternal—or rather maternalized—prelanguages), we wish to discuss Kristeva's most recent articulations in *Black Sun* of what she sees as a prelanguage that has its roots in a relation to the "primal object," the mother (66–67).[8] When Kristeva turns from her patients to a discussion of language, she employs the specifically Kleinian definition of the primal object as a *fantasy* about the mother. (Winnicott's environmental mother, the mother appropriated by Green in all her inadequacy, most obviously informs Kristeva's case histories.) As a theorist of language, Kristeva understands the problems with establishing the mother as a referent. Indeed, she acknowledges that "positing the existence of that other language and even an other language, indeed an outside-of-language" might seem to be setting up a preserve for metaphysics (66). She argues, however, that the obsession (her obsession and the melancholic's) with the mother as primal object is a requirement of Western metaphysics and subjectivity. This requirement, she insists, encourages a capacity to feel pain as a truth, a capacity that also facilitates a desire to dissolve sadness in endlessly individualized discursive performances.[9] Kristeva is particularly interested in art as the exemplary vehicle of the Western imagination. Art enables a sublimation of the excruciating pain caused by separation from the lost object—or at least it enables such a sublimation by the male artist.

Black Sun includes an analysis of four artists: Hans Holbein, Gerard de Nerval, Fyodor Dostoyevsky, and Marguerite Duras. Though her discussion of these artists follows a chronological order, Kristeva is not so much concerned with specific inscriptions of culture at different points in time as she is with Western civilization as a totalized, melancholy entity that is itself in the grip of the death drive. Of the work she discusses, Dostoyevsky's writing best exemplifies how the "unconscious might inscribe itself in a new narrative that will not be the eternal return of the death drive" (204) while Duras's writing demonstrates the devastation wrought by the failure to sublimate our terrible "passion for death" (221). Kristeva explicitly links Dostoyevsky's achievement of a rejuvenating transformation and Duras's inability to rise above her desolation to differences in masculine and feminine sexuality. Implicitly, then, Kristeva argues that we would do well to limit what seems to be the feminization of culture.[10]

If Dostoyevsky is the hero of *Black Sun*, Kristeva prepares for his emergence by first devoting a chapter to an analysis of Hans Holbein the Younger's picture, *The Body of the Dead Christ in the Tomb*, a picture that apparently made "a tremendous impression on Dostoyevsky" (107). Kristeva claims that the power of Holbein's picture, and indeed all of Holbein's art, is that it summons up a melancholic moment that is both cultural and psychic, a moment of severance—a break or hiatus. The picture represents Christ as "a man who is truly dead, of a Christ forsaken by the Father . . . and without the promise of Resurrection" (110), and so captures the affect of suffering, a particu- larly modern vision "not of glory but of endurance" (113). For Kristeva, Holbein's historical moment (as it was articulated both by "reformers and humanists") called for an intense "confrontation between men and suffering and death" (121). Holbein's particular achievement was to dignify death and to transform his disenchantment, not yet an atheistic renunciation, into beauty.

For Christians, says Kristeva, redemption comes about through the intense identification with Christ, an identification that allows the experience of death *and* resurrection. Holbein, on the other hand, demonstrates that it is possible to paint when one identifies with the moment of severance, the hiatus with no resurrection. Through his minimalist style, Holbein "fills our eyes with a vision of the invisible" (138). Isolated in the presence of Death, Holbein's people ("heroes of modern times") reveal the "sober difficulty of standing here below" with no promise of an exalted beyond (138).

Kristeva next discusses Nerval's sonnet "El Desdichado." As does Holbein's painting, this poem apparently captures the melancholic moment of severance, but Nerval resides in this moment, capturing it in great intensity and detail. Kristeva's account of Nerval's disinheritance is double-edged. Like Holbein, Nerval identifies with the Christ betrayed by the Father, but Nerval is an atheist. Kristeva makes an implicit correspondence: the less there is of God the Father, the more the feminization of the artist. While Holbein's "disenchant-ment" is visible in the desolation of the women he portrayed, Kris-teva argues that Nerval is far more in touch with the sadness of women, which he confuses with his own, and with the feminine. Thus his "disinheritance" is also his loss of "an unnameable domain" which "assumes the consistency of the archaic mother" (145). In his sonnet, Nerval plays dangerously with and against "dark asymbolia" by risking capture by that elusive Thing "necessarily lost so that this 'subject' . . . might become a speaking being" (145).

Kristeva's analysis of this sonnet follows a narrative of the emer-gence of an "I" that is always in danger of too great an identification with or captivation by the dead Thing, represented in the poem as the dead mother. To join her in death would be a solace, but the "I" also recognizes that to do so would be lethal. Nerval feverishly amasses names that do not point to a concrete referent but rather call up an "unnameable presence." Kristeva explains: "By representing that unsymbolized as a maternal object Nerval protects himself against collapsing into asymbolism" (165). Though his sonnet has the trajectory of a narrative, and so seems yet another oedipal story, it is not. Instead, his "prosodic polymorphism"—rhythms, melodies, al-literations—favors sounds and creates a "network of intensities" rather than a univocal meaning (170). In what has become a staple of Kristeva's writing on literature, a polymorphic style is linked with access to the body and resistance to the paternal Symbolic. Predict-ably, Kristeva links Nerval's style to his ability to remain in touch with the archaic maternal while still escaping its dangerous seduc-tion. According to Kristeva, Nerval's style enables a temporary tri-umph over depression.

For Kristeva, Nerval's madness is controlled through the subli-mation of his art, specifically the form and technique of his style. Dostoyevsky's enthrallment with death and suffering apparently takes even more risk, for in his work we see Nerval's "black spot" becoming a "torrent of passion, a hysterical affect if you wish . . . that imposes as ultimate truth of his characters a rebellious flesh that delights in not submitting to the Word" (177). In contrast to Holbein and Nerval, Dostoyevsky powerfully represents suffering as a primary affect, "the ultimate indication of a break that immediately precedes the subject's and the Other's becoming autonomous.... Suffering is the first or the last attempt on the part of the subject to assert his 'own and proper' at the closest point to the threatened biological unit..." (182). Dostoyevsky forges a new man with a new style that Kristeva characterizes as "the verbalization of affects," specifically the affect of suffering (178). As always, Kristeva links this suffering to femininity: the more one suffers the more one is in touch with the feminine. Thus Dostoyevsky's new man in *Crime and Punishment*, Raskolnikov, is also feminized. Kristeva quotes him as saying "I am so sad, so sad... like a woman" (*Black Sun* 196). But the male writer, unlike the depressed woman, is capable of using the resources of this feminine prelanguage of sorrow as a basis for a new discourse.

In spite of her expansive claims for Dostoyevsky's style, its "breathtaking polyphony" (*Black Sun* 177) and its revolutionary "dialogism," Kristeva never provides any textual evidence for her claims, relying instead upon a footnote to Bakhtin.[11] Indeed, though reputed to be a critic interested in avant-garde signifying systems, Kristeva now seems to prefer old-fashioned character analysis to the analysis of style. In Dostoyevsky's novels, different characters provide Kristeva with a way of discussing different defenses against suffering. The character Kirillov in *Crime and Punishment*, for instance, represents the possibility of the atheistic "suicidal terrorist" (*Black Sun* 186) who directs his aggression against himself so as to negate divinity while maintaining it. But the new man is most fully represented by the character Raskolnikov, Kristeva writes, who successfully "redirects" his hatred, turning it not upon himself but upon another "disavowed, denigrated person." This person is "an insignificant woman" (187). Yet, lest we think that Kristeva is privileging murder over suicide, men's lives over women's, Kristeva calls this sort of manic defense "contemptible" (187). Besides, as it emerges through Kristeva's analysis, Raskolnikov is really killing himself by killing the apparently "insignificant woman." Kristeva thus transforms the murder of a woman into a psychic process. Dostoyevsky "probes an essential aspect of depressive dynamics" and "brilliantly brings to the fore the identification of the depressed with the hated object" who is both the mother and the self (197).

It is important to note how little Kristeva offers in the way of cultural analysis here. Kristeva reads *Crime and Punishment* as if it offered a transparent window on to psychic processes. In her emphasis on representation as a universal allegory of psychic processes, Kristeva has lost sight of representation as a vehicle of social meanings and desires. The extent of her oversimplification of the "meaning" of *Crime and Punishment* is dramatically illustrated by comparing it to another reading of the book. In a recent article, Deborah Cameron illustrates a complex politics of representation through her discussion of responses to the discovery that Ian Brady, a serial murderer, was profoundly influenced by *Crime and Punishment*.

> Conservative commentators who have dilated on the perverseness of Brady's reading (since Dostoyevsky clearly does not endorse Raskolnikov's actions, Brady just got the meaning of the book wrong and that was his problem) entirely miss the point; nor do most of them seriously propose that *Crime and Punishment* should be banned. But those liberals who want to claim that representations have no connection with reality also miss the point. The connection is not one of cause and effect, but is rather mediated by the creation of meaning: in this case, the construction of Brady's desire, which must have been constrained (though, importantly, it was not determined in some cause-effect relation) by those cultural definitions of the erotic to which he had access. (788)

Cameron's analysis insists, as Kristeva's does not, on asking how the erotic is constituted by representations (Kristeva sees representation as simply *revealing* psychic processes). Cameron also takes into account how our desires shape our readings. We can see, then, what is missing from Kristeva's analysis. It does not seriously explore the relation between the psychic and the social nor does it consider the sexual politics of representation.

Only an interpretation insensitive to the role of representation in the construction of sexuality could find in *Crime and Punishment* a "solution, a third way between dejection and murder" (*Black Sun* 199), that celebrates classic gender types: the man redeemed by the whore with the heart of gold. Kristeva's "third way" is forgiveness. According to Kristeva, Raskolnikov learns the value of forgiveness from the prostitute, Sonia, supposedly a representation of the loving but unfaithful mother. This benevolent woman exists to enable the man to understand himself. Kristeva has nothing to say about how "woman" is here constructed. Her emphasis is entirely on the development of a new kind of man. It is not surprising, then, that when Kristeva shifts from character analysis to discuss Dostoyevsky's writing in general, woman is even more effaced. Kristeva exalts the male writer who is able to transform his suffering into a work of art with the help "of the benevolent father specific to Byzantine tradition, his affection and forgiveness" (214). Stripped of Kristeva's unconvincing historicizing, this Byzantine patriarch is Kristeva's favorite, the "father of individual prehistory."

Kristeva's sentimental evocation of Christian (specifically, Catholic Orthodox) forgiveness is an attempt to revise Melanie Klein's ideas about reparation, the stage beyond depressive anxiety. According to Klein, all symbol formation, including art, is an act of reparation. Hanna Segal has lucidly summarized Klein's analysis of reparation: " . . . symbol formation is the outcome of a loss, it is a creative work involving the pain and the whole work of mourning" (76). The Kleinian infant finds in reparation a way to repair the mother and the self. Since for Klein reparation arises in the depressive position at a stage of development before sexual difference, the sex of the infant is not emphasized in her account. For Kristeva, however, "forgiveness" is a mechanism that regenerates the male subject, especially the male artist, through the production of art. The mother as a good object, central to Klein's account of reparation, is in Kristeva's account relegated to the domain of the Thing, both a dangerous and sensuous source of affects that infuse language. And as Kristeva proceeds to a discussion of Marguerite Duras, the woman writer joins the mother in this primordial realm.

Marguerite Duras serves as the nether end of the trajectory of destruction that Kristeva argues begins with Holbein in the death of God and the possibility of severance without resurrection. The world of Duras's novels is our contemporary world, whose two great emblems are Hiroshima and Auschwitz. Kristeva explains that

> never has the power of destructive forces appeared as unquestionable and unavoidable as now, within and without society and the individual. The despoliation of nature, lives, and prop-

erty is accompanied by an upsurge, or simply a more obvious display, of disorders whose diagnoses are being refined by psychiatry—psychosis, depression, manic-depressive states, borderline states, false selves, etc. (221–22)[12]

In tune with this state of things, Duras produces what Kristeva calls "the literature of *our* illness" (258). And yet as Kristeva proceeds with her analysis it becomes clear that she believes Duras's novels are written less in response to a specific historical situation than to a more universal and "transhistorical" distress, the distress of a specifically feminine illness. Thus does Kristeva's first extended analysis of the work of a woman writer become just another case study of a woman locked in an embrace with the dead mother.

Duras's "discourse of dulled pain" captures the "malady of death" in an "aesthetics of *awkwardness*," a style both clearly less musical than that produced by Duras's male counterparts and *"noncathartic"* (*Black Sun* 225–26; Kristeva's italics). While Kristeva speaks of the male artists in a tone of reverence, if not awe—Holbein's minimalist style is "dignified" (119), "sober" (138); Nerval is "brilliantly" perceptive (169); Dostoyevsky discovers the beauty and "solemnity" of forgiveness (189)—she speaks of Duras's aesthetic practice with barely concealed contempt.

It seems that Duras's problems as a stylist reflect less the disintegration of the contemporary social fabric than what Kristeva asserts to be "a certain truth of feminine experience" (245). And given Kristeva's view of femininity, one is not surprised to hear that Kristeva believes the destructiveness and death in Duras's novels allows for no escape. Duras's texts "domesticate the malady of death, they fuse with it . . . without either distance or perspective" (227). The conclusions of these novels offer "no promise of a beyond not even the enchanting beauty of style or irony . . ." (228). Her books are like "spider webs" that hold us captive to pain and increase it without hope of redemption. Kristeva explains this phenomena by resorting again to character analysis: Duras's female characters are locked in "permanent identification with the object of mourning" (233), and, predictably, this impossible mourning for an "old love" determines them as sexually frigid. Kristeva explains that the female character in Duras's novels is unable to successfully commit matricide. While she hates and fears the mother, the daughter destroys her only to take her place. Rather than "killing" the mother, then, the daughter replicates her.

In Chodorow's notion of the reproduction of mothering, the process of replication is ambiguously situated as both oppressive (women's continuing ties to their mothers leave them without a sufficiently autonomous selfhood) and beneficial (women's ties to their mothers give them special capacities for affiliation and empathy). Kristeva's account of the reproduction of mothering, based, like Chodorow's, on an object-relations model of development, offers a much bleaker picture of mother-daughter relations. Kristeva insists on the mother's diabolical control over the daughter's subjectivity. This baleful maternal influence impedes the daughter's capacity both to speak and to feel.

As is the writing of Nerval and Dostoyevsky, Duras's writing is haunted by doubles. But Kristeva claims that Duras's doubles are qualitatively different in that they are the product of "reduplication," that is, "jammed repetition" (246) that precedes the mirror stage; thus these doubles "magnify their melancholia to the point of violence and delirium" (257). Neither Duras nor her characters (the two are constantly fused in Kristeva's analysis) achieve mastery within the Symbolic because of their overwhelming debt to the dead mother. "Never," writes Kristeva, "has the representation of cataclysm been assumed by so few symbolic means" (223). While the male artist can follow with brilliant perceptiveness the trajectory of melancholia and, finally, both give it expression and master it, Duras follows "ill-being step by step, almost in clinical fashion, without ever getting the better of it" (224).

Kristeva's analysis of Duras, then, simply serves to exemplify what she has to say about feminine sexuality and "illness." The reader who recalls the earlier case studies of women patients in Black Sun will note the resemblance of Duras's women characters, if not Duras herself, to these patients. Their speech is devitalized; they are paranoid and sexually frigid as a result of an abandonment by a mother who is consequently encrypted. Kristeva's conclusion again attempts to make of Duras a representative of her age, but the message is finally that she is an exemplary instance of the sick female. Duras, Kristeva tells us, is simply part of a historical moment that is even now being challenged by the "postmodern" (258), which is apparently closer to the "human comedy" than "to the abyssal discontent" (258–59). Since in Kristeva's scheme, women are associated with sadness and the abyss rather than with the comic, Kristeva's prophesy has the effect of suggesting that the influence of the feminine, understood now to be part of an eternal "transhistorical" cycle, has had its turn on the wheel of fortune. Soon, she suggests, an alternative will rise to replace it. Given Kristeva's way of structuring history, that alternative must inevitably be the same old thing: the affirmative male, Christian writer who is capable of sublimation.

Kristeva has usually been identified as a Lacanian analyst, but *Black Sun* demonstrates that she is profoundly influenced by André Green and object-relations theory. Because of her understanding of the radical arbitrariness of language, she appears to be far more skeptical than Green or Winnicott about locating the maternal as an origin. Instead of associating mourning and melancholia with something she explicitly labels "the dead mother complex," she pushes the source of melancholia back to an ever earlier separation that she calls primitive and biological, the "Thing." At one point, Kristeva describes the psychic inscription of this separation as "the leap from inorganic to organic matter" (176). Obviously, then, she is still concerned to locate a biological origin. This biological origin inevitably becomes the mother. For all her apparent efforts to revise Green, such as the occasional moments when she claims that the linking of the lost object to the mother is an effect of the male artist's retroactive fantasizing, she herself repeatedly assumes the link between the mother and the lost object. In her case studies, the mother is defined as *the* problem for her female patients. This way of defining the mother works to restrict the agency of women, whose language—as apparently exemplified in the work of Duras—Kristeva finds awkwardly repetitive. Revolutionary discourse is the prerogative of the male artist, not the woman writer. For Kristeva, avant-garde writing only offers the *man* a chance to be in touch with his primal femininity while safely transcending this deadly force.

Rarely in recent psychoanalytic feminism has femininity seemed more detached from cultural determinants than it does in Kristeva's account. Kristeva's books are always set up to look as if they will offer a culturally specific reading of sexual difference, but the development of difference is never explained in Kristeva's writing. In *Black Sun*, for example, Kristeva assumes originary sexual difference and by doing so refuses to acknowledge gender as an unstable, constructed category. Why is a woman less capable of matricide than a man and thus more victimized by the "dead mother complex"? Kristeva never specifically answers this question, but her argument depends on the idea that the infant girl makes an almost immediate identification with the mother. Indeed, Kristeva seems to assume that sexual difference exists at a point located even earlier than Klein's paranoid-schizoid position, which Klein says defines the infant's position in the first three months of life. Chodorow at least tries to account for the daughter's identification with the mother, attributing it to the mother's responses to the infant. As we discuss in an earlier chapter, this explanation itself deserves scrutiny because of the way it sets up the mother as origin. Our point is simply that Chodorow, unlike Kristeva, acknowledges that her notion of the daughter's maternal identification is something that she has to explain. Kristeva effectively naturalizes this process.

It is fair to say that in *Black Sun* Kristeva assumes anatomy is destiny. As we have shown, this Freudian view of sexual difference is both rearticulated and expanded in Green's article "Aggression, Femininity, Paranoia, and Reality." Drawing on the work of Green, Kristeva's *Black Sun* dramatically demonstrates the oppressiveness of object-relations discourse as it binds women to stereotypical maternal roles. The Kristevan mother is silent or hysterical, suicide or terrorist. Object-relations theorists mask their active role in perpetuating oppressive constructions of the mother by insisting that the mother is an *origin* to be explained rather than an *effect* of the analyst's own representational practices. In Kristeva's work, for example, the mother is located at the very origin of language itself. Kristeva explains that her depressed female patients suffer from an encounter with an archaic, death-bearing mother that forecloses the paternal metaphor, leaving the daughter sad and silent. Defining depression as an originary discursive condition, especially of the daughter who fails to commit matricide, is obviously oppressive to women (defined here as victims and victimizers). A signifying practice like Kristeva's, a discourse that refuses to discuss the social, political, and economic situation of women (except as symptoms of an archaic relation to a maternal object), can offer little insight into the complex sources of female depression—and little hope for a cure.[13] Further, a psychoanalysis that normalizes the notion of the mother as origin does not engage in the feminist task of destabilizing the familiar categories in which women have been confined. As we have seen, such an interrogation of familiar categories, especially of the stereotype that a woman is primarily defined through her relationship to motherhood, is difficult to undertake from within object-relations theory. Object-relations theories tell us to "Cherchez la mère": we advise a close scrutiny of this imperative, an imperative that has done more to maintain than to challenge the norms of patriarchal culture.

Postscript

If we look at how the representation of the mother evolves in object-relations theory, we see an increasing literalization of what was for Melanie Klein the phantasy world and constructs of an infant. From the Kleinian infant's fragmented, paranoid, and schizoid phantasies of a good breast and a bad breast, D. W. Winnicott develops a theory about the good and bad behavior of actual mothers. Chodorow accepts Winnicott's construct of "good enough" mothering, assuming that this category and the obligations it specifies are so necessary as to appear natural. Finally, Julia Kristeva (following André Green) conflates Klein and Winnicott: the bad breast becomes the dead mother, a fiction given life in case studies. As if this literalization of the infant's phantasies (and their projection onto actual mothers) is not disturbing enough, object-relations discourse also develops an increasingly unified conceptualization of the mother, one that stresses the mother as an origin and fixes her there, elevated for our emulation (the "good enough" mother) or approbation (the depressed mother). It is precisely the fixity of this conception, which reinforces conventional representations of women, that makes it so congenial to a conservative political agenda.[1] Feminists found in object-relations theory a strategy for creating a shared, positive identity and experience. Motherhood was revalued, though still defined in stereotypical ways, so feminist notions of women's difference became implicated in a massive backlash effort to restrict possibilities for women to "opportunities" associated with hearth and home.

We do not see any reason to assume that women are basically alike or that once they become mothers they suddenly conform to some standard "good enough." Differences between and among mothers, and even within one woman—her inconsistencies and complex allegiances—should be explored as positive resources. Such an exploration is extremely difficult to accomplish within object-relations theory. In the discourse of object relations, the female subject is represented as constructed by primary psychological processes. This focus on infantile experience precludes attention to other cultural arenas: economic, social, and linguistic.

In *Klein to Kristeva* we have only begun a larger project of mapping the ways in which powerful discourses construct femininity. The theoretical texts of object-relations theory have done much to legitimate recent feminist work on women's difference. For all the apparent variety of this work, its source in object relations seems inevitably to reduce women's difference to her maternal functions, that is, to a traditional notion of sexual difference. In other articles, we have shown how ideas drawn from object-relations theory have permeated many discourses. The Baby M case, for example, demonstrates how the representations and testimony of numerous psychological experts, well versed in the requirements of "good enough" mothering, worked to support the prerogatives of the father, William Stern, and to deny the realities of change within the family.[2]

As feminist debate shifts away from the discussion of difference, the mother will be framed in new ways. This ongoing process promises us nothing; but it may remind us—as object-relations discourse has ceased to do—that women are inscribed in a network of stories that both secures meaning and releases it. We are not all one. In the spaces between us, between the discourses that constitute us, the heterogeneous experience of women begins to emerge.

Notes

Introduction

1. In the last decade, white, psychoanalytic feminism has provided the most influential discourse about mothering. Yet alternate discourses have quietly continued to explore how culture shapes our expectations about maternal practices. Elisabeth Badinter's *Mother Love Myth and Reality: Motherhood in Modern History*, a best-seller in France that was published in the United States in 1981, offers a powerful history of changing child-care practices in France. Badinter shows that our notions of what constitutes "normal" mothering are culturally constructed. While Chodorow's *The Reproduction of Mothering* had a greater impact on American feminism than did Badinter's book, the influence of *Mother Love* can nonetheless be felt in recent work such as historian Ellen Ross's *Labor and Love in Outcast London* (Oxford: Oxford University Press, forthcoming). Women of color have also worked to understand how mothering is shaped by specific cultural conditions. See, for example, Patricia Bell-Scott et al., *Double Stitch: Black Women Write About Mothers and Daughters* (Boston: Beacon Press, 1991).

2. Throughout our text, we have adhered to Klein's spelling of *phantasy* only when specifically referring to her concepts. This spelling emphasizes the uniqueness of her view of the infant's complex unconscious life; the other object-relations theorists that we consider use the word *fantasy*.

3. For example, see Harold Bloom's *The Anxiety of Influence* (New York: Oxford University Press, 1973) and *A Map of Misreading* (New York: Oxford University Press, 1975). For a feminist critique of Bloom's reliance upon conventional genealogical hierarchies, see Doane and Hodges, *Nostalgia and Sexual Difference*, especially chapter 4.

Chapter 1

1. Recently, Klein has received more favorable attention. For example, Klein is described in much less dismissive terms in Nancy Chodorow's *Feminism and Psychoanalytic Theory* (1989) than in Chodorow's first book. Klein, Chodorow now argues, offers an "unmediated" picture of "emotions and conflicts that relations rooted in gender evoke in the child and in the child within the adult" (3). For Chodorow, Klein's ideas are still associated with the natural, the "unmediated" emotions that apparently contrast with the

more cultural view of object relations that Chodorow associates with her own position.

A recent British journal (published after we completed this chapter), *Women: A Cultural Review*, devoted an issue to Klein (1, no. 2 [November 1990]), a sign of renewed interest in her work. Still, two new collections of essays, *Between Feminism and Psychoanalysis*, edited by Teresa Brennan, and *Feminism and Psychoanalysis*, edited by Richard Feldstein and Judith Roof, do not mention Klein's work.

2. Edward Glover, "An Examination of the Klein System of Child Psychology," in his *Psychoanalytic Study of the Child*, vol. 1 (London: Imago Publishing, 1945). Quoted in Phillips, 42.

3. For readers interested in a more comprehensive account of the various schools of object-relations theory, we recommend *Object Relations in Psychoanalytic Theory* by Jay R. Greenberg and Stephen A. Mitchell. Though this book provides a useful and thorough account of object-relations theory, issues of gender are not of central concern to the authors.

4. See Ann Scott's "Melanie Klein and the Questions of Feminism" in *Women: A Cultural Review* 1, no. 2 (November 1990): 129.

5. Readers may notice that the Kleinian infant seems quite a little adult in its ability to direct aggression and construct defenses. Klein supposed that the ego is formed far earlier than Freud claimed. Almost from the beginning of its life, the Kleinian infant has a capacity for social relatedness that is manifested in reparation and even Klein's theories of early infantile aggression assume the infant's desire to protect itself from disintegration.

6. J. Rickman, ed., *On the Bringing Up of Children* (London: Kegan Paul, 1936).

7. While object-relations theorists discuss the infant's aggressiveness, maternal anger is a tabooed subject. As Marianne Hirsch points out in her article, "Maternal Anger: Silent Themes and 'Meaningful Digressions' in Psychoanalytic Feminism," maternal anger is profoundly threatening to children, analysts, and mothers themselves. Hirsch stresses that anger is an expression of subjectivity: "To be angry is to claim a place, to assert a right to expression and discourse" (82). We will discuss Hirsch's description of maternal subjectivity in the next chapter.

Winnicott discusses maternal hate in his "Hate in the Countertransference," in which he argues that "the mother hates the baby from the word go . . . even a boy" (201). Here Klein's emphasis on the infant's aggression is replaced by maternal aggression. The good mother, suggests Winnicott, turns that hate on herself, which accounts for female masochism. "A mother must be able to tolerate hating her baby without doing anything about it. She cannot express it to him. If, for fear of what she may do, she cannot hate appropriately when hurt by her child she must fall back on masochism, and I think it is this that gives rise to the false theory of a natural masochism in women" (202). Winnicott's larger point is to explain what the patient owes to the *analyst*.

8. With savage humor, Nicholas Wright's *Mrs. Klein* dramatizes a

Kleinian relationship between Melanie Klein, her daughter Melitta, and Paula Heimann (described in the play as a surrogate daughter). Given the Kleinian infant's captivity in a phantasy life that only fuels further phantasies, it is not surprising that the play provides no escape from anxious, phantasmic relations.

There is an issue here for feminists that Wright's play does not elaborate. How might we understand the public battles between Klein and her daughter? Was Melitta expressing sadistic infantile phantasies toward her mother? Was Klein a negligent mother? The story of this mother-daughter relationship seems designed to make feminists anxious because it suggests that a sisterhood between women or between mothers and daughters is not so easily attainable.

9. Denise Riley, in her excellent book, *War in the Nursery: Theories of the Child and Mother*, discusses Klein's influence on Winnicott. Her view is that despite Winnicott's reservations about Klein's stress on inborn envy and her efforts to find the origin of the child's anxieties at ever earlier moments of infancy, he never really challenges Klein's view of the infant's psychic life. "The revision of Klein which Winnicott proposed differed from the original, not by any radical conceptual rewriting, but by a shift in timing. Dangerous emotions of 'splitting' were not, for Winnicott, implanted at birth: while they still held sway in infancy, they had a different genesis in the form of 'environmentalism'—the relation with the mother" (82). Perhaps because Riley's intention is to provide a broad overview of British child psychology in the 1940s and 1950s rather than a close reading of individual theorists, she does not fully appreciate the extent to which Winnicott departs from Klein's notions of the infant, a departure that helps to explain his interest in the mother.

10. Because of Winnicott's insistence that he appreciates mothers, critics of his work have missed the regulatory power of his construction of the mother. For example, Judith Hughes, in her *Reshaping the Psychoanalytic Domain*, writes that Winnicott "regarded [the mother] as a person in *her* own right" (175). This argument, however, is made in response to a question Hughes asks herself: "Had psychoanalytic theory come full circle? Had paternal seduction simply been replaced by maternal failure?" (175). Hughes does not understand that descriptions of maternal *success* as well as of maternal failure may erase the subjectivity of the mother.

Recent neoconservative defenses of the family also celebrate the mother-child dyad. These glorifications of the mother and child, however, function to create a fiction of the immutable family designed to forestall and denigrate cultural change. And, of course, the idealization of the mother and child "naturally" at home serves to maintain patriarchal power. See Doane and Hodges, *Nostalgia and Sexual Difference*, especially chapter 6.

11. Denise Riley notes that the father's disappearance from psychoanalytic discourse "coincides with the social stress—which was indifferent to the actual numbers of absent men—on the vanishing of the father to the war" (88).

12. The following discussion of Winnicott's "The Mirror-Role of Mother

and Family" is drawn from Doane and Hodges, "Looking for Mrs. Good-mother: D. W. Winnicott's 'Mirror-Role of Mother and Family in Child Development.'"

Chapter 2

1. See, for example, Sara Ruddick's *Maternal Thinking* (Boston: Beacon Press, 1989) and Jane Flax's "Mother-Daughter Relationships: Psychodynamics, Politics, and Philosophy" in *The Future of Difference*, ed. Hester Eisenstein and Alice Jardine (Boston: G. K. Hall, 1980). An example of Robin West's work is "Jurisprudence and Gender," in *University of Chicago Law Review* 55 (1988): 1–72. Chodorow's analysis of mothering infuses much of Keller's work, for example *A Feeling for the Organism: The Life and Work of Barbara McClintock* (New York: W. H. Freeman, 1983).

2. Susan Rubin Suleiman, in her "Writing and Motherhood," describes the psychoanalytic view of motherhood as burdensome to women, but in her brief summary of Chodorow does not really question Chodorow's assumptions about what infants need or Chodorow's argument about feminine identity and motherhood. However, because of its emphasis on the troubled relation between motherhood and writing, Suleiman's important article is the starting point for Jane Gallop's critique of psychoanalysis in "Reading the Mother Tongue: Psychoanalysis and Feminist Criticism" and for Marianne Hirsch's consideration of the limits of Chodorovian literary criticism in *The Mother/Daughter Plot: Narrative, Psychoanalysis, Feminism*, which we will discuss later in this chapter.

3. While this book was being prepared for publication, we read Madelon Sprengnether's *The Spectral Mother*. While Sprengnether understands the limitations of Chodorow's argument (its inability to analyze the way object relations positions the feminine), she ignores the way in which the mother's duties are articulated in Winnicottian object-relations theory. In her book, Sprengnether both wants to uncover how important an authority the mother is (to reinstate a hierarchal relation between mother and father) *and* criticize how psychoanalysis creates a hierarchical relation between the mother and father. Her book is thus ambivalent about its own project. It also provides another example of the pervasive influence of object relations: Sprengnether cannot do without the preoedipal mother.

4. In *Gender Trouble: Feminism and the Subversion of Identity*, Judith Butler argues that the "appearance of an abiding substance or gendered self, what the psychiatrist Robert Stoller refers to as a 'gender core,' is . . . produced by the regulation of attributes along culturally established lines of coherence" (24). Butler's critique of arguments for a fixed gender identity is designed to be disruptive of the binary relation—masculinity versus femininity—that naturalizes heterosexual desire. About feminist psychoanalytic criticism, she writes that it "tends to reinforce precisely the binary, heterosexual framework that carves up genders into masculine and feminine and forecloses an adequate discussion of the kinds of subversive and parodic convergences

that characterize gay and lesbian cultures" (66). Because Chodorow accepts the idea of masculinity and femininity as opposed identities, she necessarily finds homosexuality marginal to her concerns and to feminine desire itself: "What seems to happen . . . is that most women become genitally heterosexual" (*RM* 168). Furthermore, Chodorow's argument that if fathers were primary nurturers then girl children would be more "free to individuate" (*RM* 218) suggests that girl children of lesbian couples would have problems with separating from their mothers. Chodorow recognizes this problem in an interview in *Mother Jones*. Asked what the ideal parenting situation would be, Chodorow answers: "I have argued that it's good for children to be involved with parents of both sexes. That's difficult, because I don't want to argue that it's not okay for lesbians or gay men to bring up children. If we lived in a nonsexist society, it wouldn't matter but I think that parenting is so imbued with our sexist society that it's important for children not to have to polarize masculinity and femininity and think that one is better than the other" (19). In our chapter we discuss how Chodorow's argument reproduces polarities between masculinity and femininity.

5. In an interview, Jacqueline Rose remarks: "Nancy Chodorow says quite explicitly that the boy has to make a *larger* step to become masculine because it involves externalizing himself to the domestic domain, whereas the little girl internalizes femininity and all the other things which are identified with femininity in proximity to the home in order to acquire her sexual identity. Now I think by saying this (which is also the impetus, the theoretical drive behind her book) she has turned Freud on his head, since for Freud femininity was by far the more difficult to internalize, and transformed it into a functionalism. And so that absolute discontent of femininity is lost" ("Interview" 6). Amazingly, Rose manages to avoid the word "mothering" and with it the equation of mothering and femininity that occurs in Chodorow's work.

6. Freud's "Femininity" (In *The Standard Edition of the Complete Psychological Works of Sigmund Freud*, trans. James Strachey [London: Hogarth, 1964], 22:112–35) discusses the difficulty of becoming a woman and much feminist psychoanalytic literature has elaborated on this difficulty. (The writings of Juliet Mitchell, mentioned in this chapter, provide one influential example.) Chodorow, in making the case for the ease of acquiring femininity, imagines the father as a friendly helper able to free his daughter from bondage to the mother. The problem with this account is that this friendly father is himself the fantasized product of Chodorow's nuclear family, in which both parents are nurturers. When the father is not a nurturer (the usual case), the likelihood of father-daughter incest increases because of the hierarchical and eroticized nature of the father-daughter relationship. Chodorow says that father-daughter incest takes place when "the attachment is tenuous, so there is less need to get her to internalize a taboo against incestuous involvement with him" (*RM* 157). The crucial issue that Chodorow misses here is *power*, with the result that incest is explained as the daughter's failure to incorporate a taboo rather than as an effect of the father's power and the daughter's desire and fear of it.

7. Chodorow states that "women's mothering is not an unchanging transcultural universal" (RM 32). Yet, by the end of her book when she announces that "women come to mother because they have been mothered by women" (RM 211), mothering seems to have become "an unchanging transcultural universal." In fact, in many Chodorovian analyses, cultural and historical documentation is strongly subordinated to universalizing accounts of psychological development.

8. This women's language is usually described as characterized by its use of multiple and fluid identities and its reliance on musical effects of rhythm and vocal sound. Anglo-American literary critics often find descriptions of preoedipal language a way to apparently bridge the gap between French feminists such as Heléne Cixous whose work is based in Lacanian psychoanalysis and Anglo-American object relations. See Reconstructing Desire: The Role of the Unconscious in Women's Reading and Writing by Jean Wyatt (Chapel Hill: University of North Carolina Press, 1990) for a recent example of such a project.

9. Kristeva uses the Clytemnestra/Electra story to discuss the daughter's relation to the father and the mother in About Chinese Women. Her interest is in the "father's daughters." We will discuss Kristeva's work in the next chapter.

10. Chodorow's new book, Feminism and Psychoanalytic Theory, includes an article coauthored with Susan Contratto that argues that much feminist writing demonstrates the operation of an infantile fantasy of the perfect mother. This fantasy manifests itself in idealization of the mother and, often, blame of the child. Chodorow and Contratto are aware that "models of child development" (95) shape our ideas about infantile needs and maternal omnipotence, but the authors seem to feel able to see "beyond the myths and misconceptions embodied in the fantasy of the perfect mother" (95). Our analysis of The Reproduction of Mothering suggests that Chodorow's own attachment to object-relations theory—which itself perpetuates the myth of the mother who acts selflessly on behalf of a child (who, in this construction, must seem dangerous to the mother's selfhood)—demonstrates how difficult it is to move "beyond" powerful representations of child development.

11. In her book, Hirsch writes: "I take neither the notion of 'experience' as a given nor that of 'identity' as a given . . ." (13), but she is deeply concerned to accurately "tell the story of female development" (161) in both the voices of the mother and the daughter. She suggests here that there is some grounding teleology of female development or a voice specific to the mother and another to the daughter.

Chapter 3

1. See Cynthia Chase, "Desire and Identification in Lacan and Kristeva," in Feminism and Psychoanalysis, ed. Richard Feldstein and Judith Roof. In Black Sun Kristeva does not emphasize the abject mother, mentioned by Chase, but the concept deserves some discussion. The term abjection designates a

psychic moment under sway of the death drive that occurs before libidinal drives are directed toward external objects. It has resonance with the Kleinian paranoid-schizoid position since abjection is an early position involving both aggression and splitting. Kristeva writes that abjection is constituted in relation to "maternal anguish" (*Powers of Horror* 12). The mother is in anguish over her inability to situate herself, or, in Kristeva's words, "to be satiated within the encompassing symbolic" (12). Again, we are dealing with an unhappy mother and her effect on the child; as described in *Powers of Horror*, the effect may be jouissance or pain.

2. In Lacan's work, the "objets petits autres" are those objects with the least "otherness" for the infant. This category of objects is similar to what Klein called the "part-objects," such as the breast and feces.

3. In her article, "Julia Kristeva: Take Two," Jacqueline Rose has acknowledged, though not elaborated upon, the influence of Green's work on Julia Kristeva's understanding of psychic life: "The concept of 'affect' . . . comes through André Green, a member of the Psychoanalytique de France, founded when its members split with Lacan in 1964 (Kristeva trained as an analyst with this school). Green's book *Le discours vivant* developed the concept of affect in Freud as part of a critique of Lacan's central premise that psychic life is ruled by the exigencies of representation and the linguistic sign" (24).

4. This chapter is included in a collection of Green's essays translated in English, *On Private Madness*. All of our citations of Green are from this text.

5. Kristeva defines the maternal *chora* as "a receptacle, unnameable, improbable, hybrid, anterior to meaning, to the One, to the father, and consequently maternally connoted to such an extent that it merits 'not even the rank of syllable' " (*Desire in Language* 133). This maternal receptacle, a semiotic space linked to the maternal body, recalls Winnicott's "potential space." While Kristeva takes the term *chora* from Plato, it seems likely the object-relations theory helped to shape her concept of an intermediary space shared by mother and infant, though in Kristeva's account this space is much more indeterminate linguistically and socially than any Winnicottian space.

6. Kaja Silverman, in a discussion of Kristeva's "Motherhood According to Bellini," notes that Kristeva's emphasis on primary narcissism allows her to "wrest from the mother any claim to primacy, and to install the phallus within the psyche as the absolutely privileged term . . . and gives the father a privileged position within the imaginary as well as the symbolic" (118). She goes on to point out that "the mother . . . is now not only separated from the child at the moment of the latter's entry into language, but jettisoned at the very moment at which the child accedes to its first identification, well before the mirror stage" (118). In this early work by Kristeva, Silverman detects strategies for positioning the mother that will be developed in *Black Sun*.

7. Paul Smith's critical remarks about Kristeva's reading of the Don Juan legend in *Tales of Love* also arise from a concern about the way Kristeva's more recent meditations on subjectivity and language bypass feminist interpretations. "In dealing with the Don Juan legend Kristeva claims that the

fundamental narrative of the protagonist's counting and re-counting of women is of less interest than the state into which that narrative brings him. . . . [For Kristeva], Don Juan is in quest of 'the impossible identificatory object' " (197), and this quest leads him away from morality—a realm of little usefulness in Kristeva's account—and toward the 'baroque drunkenness of signs, to their original and musical inconstancy' (Smith 97). Such a reading, Smith goes on to say, forecloses an ideological critique. As we will discuss later, Kristeva's discussions of male artists in *Black Sun* also culminate in effusions about the artifice of signs as a compensation for the lost object.

8. See, for example, Elizabeth Grosz's *Sexual Subversions: Three French Feminists;* Kaja Silverman's *The Acoustic Mirror: The Female Voice in Psychoanalysis and Cinema;* Domna Stanton's "Difference on Trial: A Critique of the Maternal Metaphor in Cixous, Irigaray and Kristeva."

9. Kristeva often makes transhistorical statements based on anecdotes about other cultures. For example, in *Powers of Horror: An Essay on Abjection,* Kristeva cites V. S. Naipaul's observation that "Hindus defecate everywhere without anyone ever mentioning, either in speech or in books, those squatting figures, because, quite simply, no one sees them" (74). Kristeva goes on to explain that this inability to represent defecation [Naipaul's authority is not questioned] suggests that in Indian society what would normally be understood as a psychotic split between the body (associated with the mother, nature, the real) and signifying practices has become socialized. In *Black Sun,* Kristeva says Chinese civilization does not posit an outside-of-language. She claims that the advantage of the Chinese model is "its mystical immanence with the world. But, as a Chinese friend recognized, such a culture is without means for facing the onset of pain" (67). Here the "Chinese friend" confers authority on Kristeva's universalizing pronouncements. Through her construction of the "Orient," Kristeva consolidates her claims about Western civilization, metaphysics, and discourse. A familiar Orientalist binarism underlies her characterizations of "West" and "East": autonomy versus plurality.

Gayatri Spivak has commented on other aspects of Kristeva's Orientalism. In her fine article, "French Feminism in an International Frame," Spivak analyzes, among other things, the Western cultural practices employed by Kristeva in *About Chinese Women.* In this book, Kristeva extols the primitive East as a source of truths about the preoedipal (and essential masculinity and femininity) while also treating the contemporary East with contempt. Spivak points out that this contempt often involves a "principled anti-feminism" (Spivak uses this phrase ironically) that understands the limits of contemporary revolutionary collectivities.

10. In *Black Sun* Kristeva's subject position is curious. Her voice often seems designed to suggest that it transcends sexual identity (hers is a privileged metadiscourse that comments from beyond time and place). Yet her preoccupation with depicting the depressed woman is a form of identification with a sorrowful female subject. Indeed Kristeva often seems to speak for this mute woman: "My pain is the hidden side of my philosophy, its

mute sister" (4). There is a curiously unresolved Hegelian dynamic to this "Kristeva," the subject as exalted and abject, master and slave.

11. See *Black Sun*, 276n.16. Kristeva is referring to Mikhail Bakhtin's *Problems of Dostoyevsky's Poetics* (Ann Arbor: University of Michigan Press, 1973).

12. André Green makes a similar statement but much more tentatively. He says that he is not sure if there really are more patients now suffering from psychoses or whether psychoanalytic theory has simply generated more interest in (and notice of) psychoses. See his introduction to *On Private Madness*, especially page 11.

13. The American Psychological Association recently issued a report, the result of a three year study by the Task Force on Women and Depression, that found that women suffer depression more than men. Women's frequent depressions are explained as primarily due to their experience of being female in our culture. The report cites stresses associated with the care of small children, poverty, and sexual and physical abuse as key factors linked with depression in women.

While it is crucial to take into account women's subordinate position in patriarchy when discussing depression (as Kristeva does not), the report of the American Psychological Association makes of culture a simple origin or referent. For Kristeva, the subject's deep-seated psychic conflicts become monolithic as a "source" for depression. Yet, it is not necessarily better to make culture a monolithic "source" for depression. To allow for more flexibility and agency for women, feminists must challenge the notion that either the subject or culture is a foundational unity that operates in a monolithic way.

Postscript

1. See our *Nostalgia and Sexual Difference: The Resistance to Contemporary Feminism* for a discussion and analysis of this phenomenon, as well as Susan Faludi's more recent book, *Backlash: The Undeclared War against American Women*.

2. See our article "Risky Business: Familialism, Ideology, and the Case of Baby M," in *differences: A Journal of Feminist Cultural Studies* 1, no. 1 (Winter 1989): 67–81.

Works Cited

Brennan, Teresa, ed. *Between Feminism and Psychoanalysis*. London and New York: Routledge, 1989.

Burgin, Victor, James Donald, and Cora Kaplan. Preface. In *Formations of Fantasy*, 1–4. London and New York: Methuen, 1986.

Butler, Judith. *Gender Trouble: Feminism and the Subversion of Identity*. New York and London: Routledge, 1990.

Cameron, Deborah. "Discourses of Desire: Liberals, Feminists, and the Politics of Pornography in the 1980's." *American Literary History* 2, no. 4 (Winter 1990): 784–98.

Chase, Cynthia. "Desire and Identification in Lacan and Kristeva." In *Feminism and Psychoanalysis*, ed. Richard Feldstein and Judith Roof, 65–83. Ithaca and London: Cornell University Press, 1989.

Chodorow, Nancy. "Beyond 'Maternal Instinct': Raising the Day-Care Generation." Interview with Laura Fraser. *Mother Jones* 13, no. 9 (November 1988): 19.

———. *Feminism and Psychoanalytic Theory*. New Haven and London: Yale University Press, 1989.

———. *The Reproduction of Mothering: Psychonalysis and the Sociology of Gender*. Berkeley: University of California Press, 1978.

Dinnerstein, Dorothy. *Mermaid and the Minotaur*. New York: Harper and Row, 1976.

Doane, Janice, and Devon Hodges. "Looking for Mrs Goodmother: D. W. Winnicott's 'Mirror-Role of Mother and Family in Child Development'." *enclitic* 1, no. 2 (Fall 1982): 51–56.

———. *Nostalgia and Sexual Difference: The Resistance to Contemporary Feminism*. New York: Methuen, 1987.

Faludi, Susan. *Backlash: The Undeclared War against American Women*. New York: Crown Publishers, 1991.

Feldstein, Richard, and Judith Roof, eds. *Feminism and Psychoanalysis*. Ithaca: Cornell University Press, 1989.

Flax, Jane. "Mother-Daughter Relationships: Psychodynamics, Politics and Philosophy." In *The Future of Difference*, ed. Hester Eisenstein and Alice Jardine, 20–40. Boston: G. K. Hall, 1980.

Gallop, Jane. "Reading the Mother Tongue: Psychonanalytic Feminist Criticism." *Critical Inquiry* 13, no. 2 (Winter 1987): 314–29.

Gardiner, Judith Kegan. "Gender, Values, and Lessing's Cats." In *Feminist*

Issues in Literary Scholarship, ed. Shari Benstock, 110–23. Bloomington: Indiana University Press, 1987.

———. "On Female Identity and Writing by Women." In *Writing and Sexual Difference*, ed. Elizabeth Abel, 177–92. Chicago: University of Chicago Press, 1982.

Garner, Shirley Nelson, Claire Kahane, and Madelon Sprengnether, eds. *The (M)other Tongue: Essays in Feminist Psychoanalytic Interpretation*. Ithaca: Cornell University Press, 1985.

Gilligan, Carol. *In a Different Voice: Psychological Theory and Women's Development*. Cambridge: Harvard University Press, 1982.

Gottlieb, Roger. "Mothering and the Reproduction of Power: Chodorow, Dinnerstein, and Social Theory." *Socialist Review* 14, no. 17 (Sept.–Oct. 1984): 92–119.

Green, André. *On Private Madness*. Madison, Conn.: International Universities Press, 1986.

Greenberg, Jay R., and Stephen A. Mitchell. *Object Relations in Psychoanalytic Theory*. Cambridge: Harvard University Press, 1989.

Grosskurth, Phyllis. *Melanie Klein: Her World and Her Work*. New York: Knopf, 1986.

Grosz, Elizabeth. *Sexual Subversions: Three French Feminists*. Sydney: Allen and Unwin, 1989.

Harding, Sandra. *The Science Question in Feminism*. Ithaca: Cornell University Press, 1986.

Hirsch, Marianne. "Maternal Anger: Silent Themes and 'Meaningful Digressions' in Psychoanalytic Feminism." *minnesota reveiw* no. 29 (Fall 1987): 81–87.

———. *The Mother/Daughter Plot: Narrative, Psychoanalysis, Feminism*. Bloomington and Indianapolis: Indiana University Press, 1989.

Hughes, Judith M. *Reshaping the Psychoanalytic Domain: The Work of Melanie Klein, W. R. D. Fairbairn, and D. W. Winnicott*. Berkeley: University of California Press, 1989.

Kahane, Claire. "Questioning the Maternal Voice." *Genders* no. 3 (Fall 1988): 82–91.

Kaplan, Ann. "Dialogue." *Cinema Journal* 24, no. 1 (Fall 1984): 40–43.

Keller, Evelyn Fox. *A Feeling for the Organism: The Life and Work of Barbara McClintock*. New York: W. H. Freeman, 1983.

Klein, Melanie. "A Contribution to the Psychogenesis of Manic-Depressive States." In *Love, Guilt and Reparation and Other Works 1921–1945*, Vol. 1 of *The Writings of Melanie Klein*, ed. R. E. Money-Kyrle, B. Joseph, E. O'Shaughnessy, and H. Segal, 262–89. London: Hogarth Press and the Institute of Psychoanalysis, 1975.

———. "The Importance of Symbol-Formation in the Development of the Ego (1930)." In *Love, Guilt and Reparation and Other Works 1921–1945*, Vol. 1 of *The Writings of Melanie Klein*, ed. R. E. Money-Kyrle, B. Joseph, E. O'Shaughnessy, and H. Segal, 219–32. London: Hogarth Press and the Institute of Psychoanalysis, 1975.

——. "Infantile Anxiety Situations Reflected in a Work of Art and in the Creative Impulse." In *The Selected Melanie Klein*, 84–94. Harmondsworth: Penguin Books, 1986.

——. "Notes on Some Schizoid Mechanisms." In *The Selected Melanie Klein*, 176–200. Harmondsworth: Penguin Books, 1986.

——. "The Oedipus Complex in the Light of Early Anxieties (1945)." In *Love, Guilt and Reparation and Other Works 1921–1945*, 370–419, Vol. 1 of *The Writings of Melanie Klein*, ed. R. E. Money-Kyrle, B. Joseph, E. O'Shaughnessy, and H. Segal, 370–419. London: Hogarth Press and the Institute of Psychoanalysis, 1975.

——. "The Psychotherapy of the Psychoses (1930)." In *Love, Guilt, and Reparation and Other Works 1921–1945*, Vol. 1 of *The Writings of Melanie Klein*, ed. R. E. Money-Kyrle, B. Joseph, E. O'Shaughnessy, and H. Segal, 233–35. London: Hogarth Press and the Institute of Psychoanalysis, 1975.

——. "Weaning." In *Love, Guilt, and Reparation and Other Works 1921–1945*, Vol. 1 of *The Writings of Melanie Klein*, ed. R. E. Money-Kyrle, B. Joseph, E. O'Shaughnessy, and H. Segal, 290–303. London: Hogarth Press and the Institute of Psychoanalysis, 1975.

Koonz, Claudia. *Mothers in the Fatherland*. New York: St. Martin's Press, 1987.

Kristeva, Julia. "About Chinese Women." In *A Kristeva Reader*, ed. Toril Moi, 138–59. New York: Columbia University Press, 1986.

——. *Black Sun: Depression and Melancholia*. Trans. Leon S. Roudiez. New York: Columbia University Press, 1989.

——. *Desire in Language*. Ed. Leon S. Roudiez. Trans. Thomas Gora, Alice Jardine, Leon S. Roudiez. New York: Columbia University Press, 1980.

——. "Freud and Love: Treatment and Its Discontents." In *A Kristeva Reader*, ed. Toril Moi, 238–71. New York: Columbia University Press, 1986.

——. "Place Names." In *Desire in Language*, ed. Leon S. Roudiez, trans. Thomas Gora, Alice Jardine, Leon S. Roudiez, 271–94. New York: Columbia University Press, 1980.

——. *Powers of Horror: An Essay in Abjection*. Trans. Leon S. Roudiez. New York: Columbia University Press, 1982.

——. "Stabat Mater." In *A Kristeva Reader*, ed. Toril Moi, 160–85. New York: Columbia University Press, 1986.

——. "Women's Time." In *A Kristeva Reader*, ed. Toril Moi, 187–213. New York: Columbia University Press, 1986.

Mitchell, Juliet. "Introduction." In *The Selected Melanie Klein*, ed. Juliet Mitchell, 9–32. Harmondsworth: Penguin Books, 1986.

——. *Psychoanalysis and Feminism: Freud, Reich, Laing, and Women*. New York: Vintage, 1974.

O'Brien, Sharon. *Willa Cather: The Emerging Voice*. New York: Oxford University Press, 1987.

Phillips, Adam. *Winnicott*. Cambridge: Harvard University Press, 1988.

Poster, Mark. *Critical Theory of the Family*. New York: Seabury Press, 1980.

Riley, Denise. *War in the Nursery: Theories of the Child and Mother.* London: Virago Press, 1983.

Rose, Jacqueline. "Interview 1982." *m/f* no. 8 (1983): 3–16.

———. "Julia Kristeva: Take Two." In *Coming To Terms,* ed. Elizabeth Weed, 17–33. New York: Routledge, 1989.

Rose, Jacqueline, and Juliet Mitchell, eds. *Feminine Sexuality: Jacques Lacan and the école freudienne.* New York: Norton, 1982.

Ruddick, Sara. *Maternal Thinking.* Boston: Beacon Press, 1989.

Scott, Ann. "Melanie Klein and the Questions of Feminism." *Women: A Cultural Review* 1, no. 2 (November 1990): 127–34.

Segal, Hanna. *Introduction to the Work of Melanie Klein.* New York: Basic Books, 1974.

Silverman, Kaja. *The Acoustic Mirror: The Female Voice in Psychoanalysis and Cinema.* Bloomington: Indiana University Press, 1988.

Smith, Paul. "Julia Kristeva et al.; or, Take Three or More." In *Feminism and Psychoanalysis,* ed. Richard Feldstein and Judith Roof. Ithaca: Cornell University Press, 1989.

Spivak, Gayatri. "French Feminism in an International Frame." *In Other Worlds: Essays in Cultural Politics,* 134–53. New York: Methuen, 1987.

Spock, Benjamin. *Baby and Child Care.* New York: Pocket Books, 1976.

———. Introduction. In *Babies and Their Mothers,* ed. Clare Winnicott, Ray Shepherd, Madeleine Davis, vii–xii. Reading, Mass.: Addison-Wesley, 1987.

Sprengnether, Madelon. *The Spectral Mother: Freud, Feminism, and Psychoanalysis.* Ithaca: Cornell University Press, 1990.

Stanton, Domna. "Difference on Trial: A Critique of the Maternal Metaphor in Cixous, Irigaray and Kristeva." In *The Poetics of Gender,* ed. Nancy K. Miller, 157–82. New York: Columbia University Press, 1986.

Suleiman, Susan Rubin. "Writing and Motherhood." In *The (M)other Tongue: Essays in Feminist Psychoanalytic Interpretation,* ed. Shirley Nelson Garner, Claire Kahane, and Madelon Sprengnether, 352–77. Ithaca and London: Cornell University Press, 1985.

Williams, Linda. " 'Something Else Besides a Mother': *Stella Dallas* and the Maternal Melodrama." *Cinema Journal* 24, no. 1 (Fall 1984): 2–27.

Winnicott, D. W. "The Antisocial Tendency." *Through Paediatrics to Psychoanalysis,* 306–15. London: Tavistock, 1958.

———. "The Baby as a Going Concern." *The Child and the Family,* 13–17. London: Tavistock, 1957.

———. "The Development of the Capacity for Concern." *The Maturational Processes and the Facilitating Environment,* 73–82. New York: International Universities Press, 1965.

———. "This Feminism." *Home is Where We Start From: Essays by a Psychoanalyst,* 183–94. New York and London: Norton, 1986.

———. "Getting to Know Your Baby." *The Child and the Family,* 7–12. London: Tavistock, 1957.

———. "Hate in the Countertransference." *Through Paediatrics to Psychoanalysis*, 194–203. London: Tavistock, 1958.

———. "A Man Looks at Motherhood." *The Child and the Family*, 3–6. London: Tavistock. 1957.

———. "The Mirror-Role of Mother and Family." *Playing and Reality*, 111–18. New York: Basic Books, 1971.

———. "The Mother's Contribution to Society." *Home is Where We Start From: Essays by a Psychoanalyst*, 123–27. New York and London: Norton, 1986.

———. "A Personal View of the Kleinian Contribution." *The Maturational Processes and the Facilitating Environment*, 171– 78. New York: International Universities Press, 1965.

———. *Playing and Reality*. New York: Basic Books, 1971.

———. "Primary Maternal Preoccupation." *Through Paediatrics to Pyschoanalysis*, 300–305. London: Tavistock, 1958.

———. *The Spontaneous Gesture: Selected Letters of D.W. Winnicott*. Ed. Robert Rodman. Cambridge: Harvard University Press, 1987.

———. "Their Standards and Yours." *The Child and the Family*, 87–91. London: Tavistock, 1957.

———. "What about Father." *The Child and the Family*, 81–86. London: Tavistock, 1957.

Index

DATE DUE

APR 2 9 1996			
	DEC 1 4 1996		
JAN 1 7 1996			
			Printed in USA